ANTISEMITISM
IN
AMERICA

ANTISEMITISM
IN
AMERICA

A WARNING

SENATOR
CHUCK SCHUMER

with JOSH MOLOFSKY

GRAND
CENTRAL

New York Boston

Grand Central Publishing

Hachette Book Group

1290 Avenue of the Americas, New York, NY 10104

grandcentralpublishing.com

@grandcentralpub

First Edition: March 2025

Grand Central Publishing is a division of Hachette Book Group, Inc. The Grand Central Publishing name and logo is a registered trademark of Hachette Book Group, Inc.

The publisher is not responsible for websites (or their content) that are not owned by the publisher.

The Hachette Speakers Bureau provides a wide range of authors for speaking events. To find out more, go to hachettespeakersbureau.com or email HachetteSpeakers@hbgusa.com.

Grand Central Publishing books may be purchased in bulk for business, educational, or promotional use. For information, please contact your local bookseller or the Hachette Book Group Special Markets Department at special.markets@hbgusa.com.

Print book interior design by Marie Mundaca

Library of Congress Cataloging-in-Publication Data has been applied for.

ISBNs: 9781538771624 (hardcover), 9781538771648 (ebook)

Printed in the United States of America

LSC-C

Printing 1, 2025

For the five generations of Schumers in America—from my Grandpa Jack to my three precious grandchildren, Noah, Eleanor, and Henry—and for the generations yet to come.

CONTENTS

"For not only one [enemy] has risen up against us to destroy us, but in every generation they rise up to destroy us. But the Holy One, Blessed be He, delivers us from their hands."

—Translation of "Vehi Sheamada," a passage from the Haggadah, the sacred text of Passover (first appearance in the early eighth century)

"Antisemitism is a light sleeper."

—Conor Cruise O'Brien, Irish writer and diplomat (1986)

INTRODUCTION

I never thought that I would write a book like this. For one thing, I never thought antisemitism would rise to the level that it has today in America. But also, like many Jewish-Americans, despite (or maybe because of) my public profile, I have always had mixed feelings about how strongly I should advertise or lean into my Jewish identity. For most of my career, I have just tried to be myself. I've told my colleagues and especially fellow Democratic candidates that in order to succeed in politics, they have to be who they truly are. Voters can smell inauthenticity, the way bloodhounds track a scent. I have a maxim I tell any candidate for public office. *I'm from Brooklyn*, I say. *Sometimes it hurts me; sometimes it helps me. But I know if I tried to be anything else, I would be worse than whatever I am.* I've always understood, implicitly, that when I say "Brooklyn," I also mean "Jewish."

But was it my job to represent our community in the United States? When I was younger, I felt no strong desire or need to speak out on behalf of Jewish-Americans. I might have worked on issues related to Jews and Israel, but people often thought of me as more outwardly Jewish than I actually was. Over my first decade in Congress, I represented Brooklyn, but in 1992, I was redistricted partially into Queens. When I was campaigning to meet the new voters in Queens on Austin Street in Forest Hills, a predominantly Jewish neighborhood, a lady wandered over to me.

In typical Jewish fashion, she skipped the pleasantries. "You're Congressman Schumer," she declared. "I read in the *Queens Tribune* that you're my new Congressman. I'm so glad. I've never met you in person, but I watch C-SPAN religiously and I'd like to pay you a compliment. You have more courage than any of the other members of Congress."

And I said, "Well, thank you, ma'am. You know, there are four hundred and thirty-five of them. Some are no-goodniks, I admit that, but some are very estimable people. What makes you say that I, out of all the four hundred and thirty-five, have the most courage?"

She said, "Well, as I said, I watch C-SPAN all the time. And when you rise to your feet to speak on the floor of the House of Representatives, you're the only one who has the courage to wear a yarmulke."

I said, "Thank you, ma'am, but it's obvious you've never met me."

I bent my head down to show her the appetizer-plate-sized bald spot on the crown of my head.

"It's not a yarmulke," I said.

Being Jewish brought meaning to my personal and political life, but it was an identity that could be worn lightly. No doubt, people thought of me as Jewish, but confusion over my hair loss aside, there was no great burden of Jewish leadership on my shoulders. There were many others, more senior, more powerful, who could take up that cudgel.

Still, as my career continued in the House, I felt a desire to bring a greater degree of my heritage into my public life. I noticed that many members really enjoyed the weekly Christian prayer breakfast. I felt that Jewish members should have one as well, so I decided to help lead a study group for Jewish representatives. We would meet every other Thursday at lunchtime. To get us started, I invited a rabbi I was close to at the time—Rabbi Jay Marcus of Young Israel of Staten Island—to lead a discussion about that week's Torah portion over a kosher spread. We would talk about the issues of the day and how they related to religious teachings or Jewish history, the intersection between the secular and the sacred. What were the origins of the Jewish holiday that week or that month? What themes or lessons could we draw from it? We had Passover and Hanukkah celebrations, even a congressional Sukkah to celebrate the Jewish harvest festival. We also held political discussions and ideological debates. *What was the Jewish attitude,* we might ask ourselves or the rabbi, *toward war, poverty, liberty, or charity?* I remember one of the meetings was about the Bush administration's response to the crisis in Kuwait after Saddam Hussein's invasion—the event that precipitated the 1991 Gulf War. We investigated our own feelings and what the Torah would say about our obligation as Jews when confronted with a decision as weighty as sending Americans into war. On many issues, we wanted to hear both sides, to debate and sometimes argue, not so different from how our families might have argued at home on Shabbat. On one occasion, members asked to wheel a television into the study group so everyone could listen to a speech by Secretary of State James Baker criticizing Israel.

When I got to the Senate in 1998, I continued the tradition. I also found myself getting up in our caucus meetings and feeling more comfortable sharing stories about my family, which was often encouraged as a way for the older senators to get to know newer members. I remember the first time I told the story of my great-grandfather.

"He was a well-known rabbi in a small village in Eastern Europe called Chortkiv," I began. "He believed devoutly in the Bible, and the first commandment in the Bible is what God told Adam and Eve: Be fruitful and multiply. So my great-grandfather had eighteen children, all with one wife. The Jews at the time were not allowed to be artisans or tradesmen or hold other professions, so all my great-grandfather did was study. Because they were poor, the youngest three were sent to America, including my grandfather, Jacob."

"Eighteen children!" interjected Byron Dorgan, a droll Midwesterner and senator from North Dakota. "He wasn't just studying!"

Ever since, when I tell the story of my family, I always note that my great-grandfather took the commandment given by God to Adam to "be fruitful and multiply" a bit too seriously.

In my early years in the Senate, I thought these interactions were good bonding experiences. They were examples of congressional camaraderie, workplace humor. But recently I've found them much more meaningful. They were examples of deeper feelings I had about imparting the story of the Jewish people to my friends and colleagues. I found that sharing my own story not only made me feel better understood and more accepted by my colleagues, it also enabled me to feel better about myself as a Jewish person—that I was doing my part to communicate aspects of our historical struggle and helping explain how Jewish-Americans might view certain issues in light of our heritage.

The first congressional delegation I led as Senate Majority Leader was in early 2023. Intentionally, it included a trip to Israel and also to Germany for the Munich Security Conference, where we sought to bolster our NATO allies and our commitment to Ukraine. As we were planning the trip, I arranged to add a visit to the Dachau concentration camp in Germany and to Yad Vashem, the Holocaust memorial and history museum, in Jerusalem. At Dachau, I walked with eight of my colleagues, most of whom were not Jewish, in total silence, through the gas chamber and crematoria, where thousands of souls were murdered. At Yad Vashem, we laid a wreath in the Hall of Remembrance. At both stops, in discussions with my colleagues, I heard the total conviction in their voices that humanity must never again let such despicable evil happen. I had no doubt that they would feel this way, but it was moving to see their understanding of Jewish culture and history—even the most difficult parts—deepen, as mine did, when I had visited those sites for the first time.

The October 7 attack occurred later that year. When I visited the shell-shocked country of Israel in the immediate aftermath, I felt that something must change about my responsibility as a Jewish leader in America. As the volume of protest and debate grew in the United States in the weeks and months that followed, and the situation in Gaza kept getting worse and worse because of the war, I felt pulled in multiple directions: as someone concerned about the rising tide of antisemitism; as someone who believes passionately in the need for the state of Israel; as someone who deplores the suffering of innocents, wherever they live; and as someone who worries about the future of the Jewish state, which is becoming increasingly isolated from much of the rest of the world. I sensed, too, that there was a great deal of confusion and pain about what was happening in America, among both Jewish and non-Jewish communities. The issues at hand were complex, hard to talk about, and in some cases wrenching. What could I do to help bring context and clarity? What was my duty as a political leader and as a Jewish-American? These were the kinds of questions I would have liked to ask my Jewish study group.

My staff in the Senate reasoned that engaging on these issues was politically risky and they advised against making lengthy public remarks on either antisemitism or the situation in the Middle East. I understood where they were coming from, and their assessment was probably correct: There was a great deal of political risk. I also felt uncertain, even inadequate. But as the first Jewish majority leader and highest-elected Jewish official in American history, I felt I had to act. In past years, I might have found myself identifying more with the sentiment expressed by Moses when God commands him to lead the Jewish people out of Egypt. *You can't mean me,* Moses thinks. *Surely there are others more suited to the task.* But here I was. I thought to myself, *Chuck, you are certainly no Moses. You are no great Jewish sage or scholar, you are no King Solomon or Maimonides or Elie Wiesel, but for better or for worse, you are here, and you ought to try to do some good.* Whatever the risks, I decided that I had to speak out: on antisemitism in America, the war in Gaza and the obstacles to peace, even the messy political realities of modern Israel. So that is what I have done.

It's not such a brave step for a United States senator to use their platform to draw attention to issues they care about, even politically risky ones. But I share these reflections because I have sensed that many of my Jewish friends are struggling with how to respond to this new feeling of foreboding for Jews in America. I have met young Jewish families in New York who send their kids to Jewish day schools, alarmed now that private security guards or armed police officers have been asked to stand outside the front doors where they drop their kindergartners off each morning. I have met with Jewish student groups who feel threatened on campus and personally devastated by the thought that their friends now believe awful things about them just because they are Jewish. Many of them are as sensitive to the suffering in Gaza as their peers who protest—some of them protest themselves—but they fear that speaking out about their experiences as Jews on campus would only invite criticism or make themselves a target. There are many Jews I've spoken to in the past year who have quietly told me that while they believe antisemitism is a growing problem, it's difficult to talk about without opening a can of worms—without addressing Islamophobia or racism or competing narratives in the Middle East.

To all of them I would say: It is never wrong to speak out about antisemitism. It need not be compared in scale or severity to other hatreds, and addressing it does not diminish in importance or urgency any other issue. Antisemitism is worthy of concern and attention in its own right, and it is as categorically wrong as any form of racism or bigotry. I hope that my decision to speak out will give courage and cover for others to do the same, because the threat of antisemitism will not subside if it is ignored or minimized. History has proven otherwise.

THE DAY I became minority leader of the United States Senate, my father, Abe, and my mother, Selma, came down to Washington from New York to sit in the gallery to listen to my first speech. It was January 2017. Only a few weeks later, Donald Trump would be inaugurated as the forty-fifth president of the United States. I remember feeling a sense of awe—not a sense of the "awesome," as my daughters would say to me when they were little, "Daddy, this is so awesome"—but of biblical awe, the angels trembling in awe as they stood before God. That was how I felt about the responsibilities that came with reaching the penultimate peak of my political career. But on that day, though it was little noted at the time, I also became the highest-elected Jewish official in American history, the son of a humble Jewish man who ran his own father's exterminating business and his loving, strong-willed housewife.

Looking back, the lack of fanfare around such a milestone for Jewish-Americans was, in fact, the whole point of American democracy. Jews had become so integrated into the fabric of American life that the ascension of a Jewish-American to the leadership of a Senate caucus was hardly an earth-shattering moment.

Four years later, I became the majority leader of the Senate in altogether different circumstances. That day, I was in a windowless room. It was January 6, 2021. The four congressional leaders had been ushered into a secured location, and we watched the events unfolding on television. A mad band of rioters and insurrectionists were stalking the halls of the US Capitol looking for "Crazy Nancy" and "the Big Jew."

Something is happening in America. There are recently empowered forces at work on the right and on the left that are tearing at the fabric of our multiethnic, pluralistic society. In our current moment, those forces have resulted in the explosion of many kinds of hatred. One particular kind of hatred, antisemitism, an ancient poison in the world, is what I intend to focus on. As a third-generation American Jew, and the relative of Jews who were murdered for being Jewish, this subject—this danger—hits very close to home.

While I have been a Jewish figure for my entire political life, fortunately I have rarely experienced antisemitism personally, and I believed the same was true for most Jewish-Americans of my generation. America has, by and large, been a tolerant and welcoming place. Save for some terrible events, perpetrated by white supremacists, political extremists, and other outliers, violence against Jews because they were Jewish was exceedingly rare. But in the last ten years, a lot has changed.

For the first time in my life, widespread antisemitism is a serious problem in America, and it's getting worse. Jewish-Americans are 2 percent of the US population, and at last count, according to the FBI, the target of 68 percent of all religion-based hate crimes. In 2017, in Charlottesville, Virginia, at a white supremacist rally protesting the proposed removal of a Confederate statue, the demonstrators chanted "Jews will not replace us." The following year, at a synagogue in Pittsburgh, a man gunned down eleven Jews at prayer. Incidents of bullying and harassment of Jews, both online and offline, on and off college campuses, have dramatically increased. So has the defacement of Jewish-owned businesses, schools, community centers, and houses of worship. And that was before Hamas, a terrorist group that runs Gaza, crossed the Israeli border one October morning to pillage, rape, kidnap, and murder innocent Jews, with little children among the victims.

Since that date, and the subsequent Israeli response, a new wave of antisemitism in America has been unleashed. Hate crimes against Jewish-Americans have skyrocketed. The Anti-Defamation League counted nearly 3,300 incidents of antisemitism in the three months following the October 7 massacre. During the same period a year prior, 712 such incidents were recorded. A letter sent recently to the governing body of California's university system by multiple Jewish organizations noted that on college campuses across the state, antisemitic incidents were up more than 2000 percent since October 7. And according to a report by the American Jewish Committee, 63 percent of American Jews feel that their place in American society is less secure than it was a year ago.

Even more alarming has been the response from certain segments of American society to the October 7 attack. Just a few days after, while the dead bodies of more than a thousand Jewish Israelis were still warm, and after two hundred had been carried as hostages into Gaza, including several American Jews, some activists were characterizing the brutal terrorist attack as justified. At Harvard, my alma mater, more than thirty student organizations signed a statement calling the Israeli regime "entirely responsible" for the attack. And the months since October 7 have brought too many examples—far too many—of overt antisemitism: American Jews being harassed, attacked, and villainized simply for being Jewish.

What has happened in America over the past few decades that created such fertile ground for the rapid increase in antisemitism? What political, social, international, and technological forces have brought the underlying sentiment of antisemitism out into the open? What misunderstandings about Jewish identity, about history, and about Israel have led to this moment? This book seeks to answer these questions.

More pointedly, it seeks to sound an alarm. I've noticed a significant disparity between how my Jewish friends regard the rise of antisemitism and how many of my non-Jewish friends regard it. For many non-Jewish people, the antisemitism we're seeing today is certainly troubling, but is not alarming. They don't deny it's a problem, but they don't see it as a priority, an urgent crisis. If you asked them to list the biggest challenges facing our country, very few would add antisemitism to the list, let alone place it near the top. To many Jewish people, however, the rise of antisemitism is a five-alarm fire that must be run toward and extinguished. On my lapel, I now often wear a pin in the shape of a blue square alongside a pin of the American flag. The blue square is a symbol of the fight against antisemitism and the campaign led by Robert Kraft's foundation to raise awareness of the danger it poses to Jews around the world. More Americans must understand the gravity of this danger.

Why? First, because it threatens not only Jewish safety and security, important as that is, but also because antisemitism threatens America's national security. It fuels extremism, online and offline, as well as domestic terrorism. America's intelligence agencies have assessed that domestic terrorism rooted in white supremacy and antisemitism is the greatest threat to homeland security today. Antisemitism even puts our democracy at risk. If growing numbers of Americans start believing that Jews secretly control our government, for example, they may stop believing that elections matter, or that democracy is working to advance their interests. History teaches us that once a society starts to turn on its Jewish members, the situation tends to get worse and worse, and expressions of hatred and bigotry against other marginalized groups become more virulent as well. Our State Department often gauges the level of antisemitism in a foreign country to measure how at risk that country is for democratic decline or even societal collapse. Antisemitism is often the canary in the coal mine, the flashing red warning sign at the beginning of democracy's end. Ultimately, antisemitism threatens not only Jewish society, but American society.

Antisemitism is often misunderstood. It is like other prejudices in some ways, but in many ways it is strange and distinct. It has a long, dark history, and over centuries of expression, it has taken many different forms. We need to understand it, in its ancient, modern, and contemporary contexts, in order to fight it. If more of our non-Jewish friends understood the history of the Jewish people, they might be more worried about its resurgence, which to many Jews feels like a breath away. As the Irish writer Conor Cruise O'Brien once said, "Antisemitism is a light sleeper."

This book is not intended to be a comprehensive history of antisemitism, or the Jewish people or the Middle East. Nor is this book intended to be a work of reportage, a compilation of all the recent examples of antisemitism in America and around the world. Instead, this book is a personal and political history of the Jewish people in America through my eyes, informed by my experiences, and how I have come to understand antisemitism in world history and American society.

At its core, this book is a warning—that antisemitism is surging, on our streets and in our schools and everywhere you look online. And if America fails to understand its context and history, if America's darker impulses ultimately overwhelm its better angels, an age-old truth will prove true once again: that antisemitism will grow in virulence, and eventually could lead to violence against Jews, and a rise in bigotry and hate across all parts of American society.

My name—Schumer—comes from the Hebrew word "shomer," which means "guardian" or "watchman." My ancestors were the watchers on the walls of a Jewish ghetto in Eastern Europe, there to alert the community to danger. I believe it is my duty to alert our country to the rising tide of antisemitism, to clarify how it can be identified and how it can be stopped. To be, as my forefathers once were, a shomer on the wall.

CHAPTER 1

WHAT IS ANTISEMITISM?

Antisemitism" is a complex term about a very simple idea. And yet sometimes our national dialogue about the subject can get muddled. Is being Jewish only a matter of faith and antisemitism is, therefore, religious intolerance: a conflict over whose God is true and whose prophets are false? Is it an age-old way of people expressing jealousy, picking scapegoats, and blaming problems on someone else? Or is antisemitism indicative of something deeper and darker, the human instinct for hatred of the "other"? And have Jews, almost always the "other" in societies in which they've lived, become the object of that hatred? How closely related is antisemitism to the criticism of Israel as a Jewish homeland? And where is the line to be drawn between legitimate criticism of the Israeli government and criticism that many Jews consider to be motivated by antisemitism?

Is antisemitism even the relevant term for our times? Wasn't it some old European disease, the driving force of historical atrocities that culminated in the Holocaust, something to be studied and dissected at universities? Or has this poisonous flower taken root in America and elsewhere today, creating a new urgency to understand and rebut it?

A decade ago, many Jewish-Americans felt that while antisemitism was something to be wary about, it was largely an aspect of an earlier and less enlightened time. We assumed that memories of the Holocaust, and that educating younger generations about its horrors, would make modern-day societies recoil from anything that resembled antisemitism, and keep most people and governments on guard against its threat. That has proven to be wishful thinking.

We need to update our conception of the term. Americans need to understand what it means to be Jewish, and not only how antisemitism operated throughout history, but how it is expressed today—with our technology, in our culture, and in our politics. Dangerous ideas on the political right and the political left, some old and some new, are contributing to a rise in antisemitism in America. Social media has exploded its reach, making it easier for extremists, antisemites, and bigots to convene with one another and spread hate. Geopolitical events like the October 7 terrorist attack against Israel, the resulting war in Gaza, and the ensuing conflict over that war have triggered a rise in antisemitism and foreshadow forces that could fuel antisemitism for decades to come. We'll examine these factors and what they portend.

The word "antisemitism" first appeared in 1879. The German journalist, politician, and agitator Wilhelm Marr coined the term to describe anti-Jewish campaigns in Germany in the late 1800s, which were growing in strength. There were other German words to describe a fear or dislike of the Jewish religion, but Marr wasn't concerned with religious objections. He wanted a new word to describe an opposition, in general, to the Jewish people. Marr believed that ethnic Germans were locked in a war against the Jews, who in his mind wielded too much power over German finance and industry. If Jewish emancipation in Germany were allowed to continue, Marr predicted it would result in "the end of the German people." The man who invented the term "antisemitism" went on to found the "League of Antisemites," a movement established solely on the basis of anti-Jewish beliefs. For Wilhelm Marr, "antisemitism" was something to which societies should aspire.

The term stuck. Even though we rarely use words like "Semite" or "semitic"—which refer to people who speak ancient Middle Eastern languages such as Hebrew, Arabic, or Aramaic—the term "antisemitism" has come to describe the history of political, racial, religious, social, and economic forms of discrimination against Jews, going back more than five thousand years. Jewish people carry these five millennia of antisemitism and subsequent persecution on their backs, wherever they go.

Like other kinds of hatred, antisemitism is not rational. It feels like a force of nature, a law of the universe, like it was never explicitly created and can never fully be destroyed. It can manifest itself in different ways: in stereotypes and biases and prejudices, along political and religious dimensions. But it is not an argument about whether Jesus is the one true savior, or Muhammad, or Hare Krishna, or any other deity. It is not really about what Jews believe, politically, or how much power

Jews have in a given society. Jews have suffered antisemitism for being capitalists and for being communists, for being too religious and for being too secular, during periods when Jews have been successful and when Jews have been destitute and marginalized, though it can be particularly pronounced after Jews have achieved a measure of wealth or achievement in a society. Nor is antisemitism specific to any one country or time period. Antisemitism is global and it is timeless. It is the hatred of a people and their heritage. It doesn't matter all that much how religious you are, how much custom you follow, or which country you're from. If you have a Jewish name or Jewish parent or grandparent, people who hate Jews will hate you, too. Antisemitism does not discriminate. To the antisemite, all Jews wear that invisible yellow Star of David on their coats.

In other words, antisemitism is a long-enduring form of racism, one of the world's oldest and most powerful types. Scholars of great renown have studied its history and offered possible explanations for its origins: demographic, sociological, political, philosophical, and psychological. To some, antisemitism almost defies explanation. But the best explanation is the simplest one.

Antisemitism means hating Jewish people and all things Jewish.

Antisemitism just *is*. Has been. Will always be.

CHAPTER 2

WHAT DOES IT MEAN
TO BE JEWISH?

In order to understand antisemitism, first one must try to understand the complexities of the Jewish experience. What does it even mean to be Jewish anyway? Many things, it turns out. It's a religion, yes, but also a heritage, a lineage, an oral tradition, a culture, a cuisine, a language, and a literature. There's no one right way to be Jewish, no strict formula. In my life, being Jewish most closely resembles the feeling of being part of a tribe. Of a people. In that sense, I believe that my upbringing has much in common with that of many other Jewish-Americans of my generation; and that while there are many ways to be Jewish, my story is typically representative of the Jewish-American story.

I was born on Thanksgiving Day in 1950. My family lived in Midwood, Brooklyn, and when my mom went into labor at about six that morning, my dad helped her into our Packard and drove to the now-shuttered French hospital in Midtown Manhattan, where she was to give birth. (When I was older, I wondered why an order of French nuns had built a hospital in Midtown.) After my father settled my mom in about 8:30 a.m., instead of going to the waiting room to bide his time with the other expectant fathers chomping their cigars, as fathers were expected to do in those days, he, being the free spirit he sometimes was, wandered over to the Macy's Thanksgiving Day Parade, which was a few blocks from the hospital. He watched it in its entirety. I was born midmorning, and he showed up at the hospital hours later in the afternoon, precipitating the first fight my parents had over me. They had seventy-two happy years of marriage, so it couldn't have done too much damage.

Our part of Brooklyn was dominated by squat, two-family brick houses. Near everyone had just come back from the Second World War, gotten married, had kids. I was part of the baby boom. The neighborhoods in those days were relatively segregated, and there were still some that prohibited Jewish residents, like Breezy Point, a beach community. But our area of Brooklyn was a mix of cultures. We lived alongside several Jewish families, but also a good number of Irish, Italian, and Polish families. Our best friends were the Tarricones next door, Tony (Italian, of course) and Mary (Irish, of course), who used to invite us over for dinner and serve baked potatoes slathered in obscene amounts of butter. To this day, our family makes what we call "Mary-style potatoes." On our block remained one solitary WASP, Mr. Leopold, who hadn't yet had the chance to move out to the suburbs.

The neighborhood was part of the American experiment.

We were the sons and daughters, grandsons and granddaughters of immigrants who came to this country from far-flung places and found themselves made anew. We each faced obstacles and discrimination, but we were able to take advantage of opportunities never afforded to our parents. Alongside a sense of community pride in whatever ethnic group you came from, there was a very deeply felt sense of American pride. People who came to America dirt-poor like my grandfather found their descendants vaulted into the great, burgeoning middle class that typified postwar America. They were grateful that America provided ladders they could climb to make it into the middle class. For instance, many of my Jewish friends' parents and grandparents were policemen, because it was seen as an honest profession with good, reliable pay; and because hiring was based on a written entrance exam rather than an interview, it was harder to discriminate against Jews. According to the Shomrim Society, the NYPD's organization for Jewish members, in 1939, 33,000 people took the entrance exam, and 1,440 received a passing grade. One-third of them were Jews.

The rise of various immigrant groups in the late '50s and early '60s made us all feel like we were part of the same grand American project, but it didn't completely dissolve the bonds of identity. The melting pot is the metaphor of choice for multiethnic America, especially New York. But rather than losing our individual histories, traditions, and mannerisms in some new, uniform soup, we kept our distinct identities and moved forward parallel to one another; less of a melting pot and more of a sandwich with multiple layers of ingredients. Each item has its own distinct flavor, but the combination tasted better when they were stacked on top of one another.

Our family's Jewishness didn't take painstaking discovery. It was always present, like water to a fish. Still, it felt like something that distinguished us from others. You knew you were Jewish, and you knew it was something special, with positives and negatives. When I was growing up, it wasn't weird for my parents to say about a friend or colleague: "You know, he's Jewish." Or just as importantly, "He's not Jewish."

We had Jewish heroes: Jonas Salk, Albert Einstein, the boxers Barney Ross and Max Baer, who wore trunks embroidered with the Star of David. Only a few decades earlier, Jewish boxers were world champions in four out of the eight weight divisions. It was a fact that my friends and I could all recite. The Dodgers pitcher Sandy Koufax was the hero of heroes, a Zeus in the Jewish-American pantheon, particularly for us in Brooklyn because he'd gone to a nearby high school, Lafayette. To us, Koufax exploded the myth that Jews were weak and could be pushed around. That he was a star athlete—not a math genius or scientist or chess player—expanded what America thought Jews could be and also who we thought we could become. Not only was Koufax a transcendent talent in the sport that dominated America's consciousness, the sport that in a sense symbolized America, but he was proudly and openly Jewish. When he refused to pitch on Yom Kippur in the 1965 World Series opener—whether you were religious or not—your Jewish heart swelled with a pride that you knew all other Jews, and only other Jews, felt.

Like the Greek myths, stories were passed down to us. My parents' generation must have felt those same swollen hearts when they were told the story of Isidor and Ida Straus, the Jewish owners of Macy's. They were among the most well-known and richest families on the *Titanic* (John Jacob Astor was the richest; Benjamin Guggenheim took silver), and beloved among the Jewish immigrant community in New York for their philanthropy.

After the *Titanic* struck the iceberg and passengers and crew were rushing to the upper decks to get onto the lifeboats, the instructions from the captain were to evacuate the women and children first. When Isidor Straus reached the decks, the steward, recognizing Isidor's name and history of charity, offered him a seat on a lifeboat to accompany Ida.

He flatly refused. "No, the women and children go first."

The steward turned and beckoned to his wife, Ida.

"I will not be separated from my husband," she reportedly said, turning to Isidor. "We've been together for forty years. Where you go, I go. As we have lived, so will we die. Together."

She was paraphrasing the Book of Ruth, from the Old Testament. "Don't urge me to leave you or to turn back from you," Ruth says. "Where you go, I will go, and where you stay I will stay. Your people will be my people and your God my God." (My daughter Alison included the passage in her wedding ceremony to her partner, Elizabeth.)

Ida gave her fur coat to her maid, an Englishwoman named Ellen Bird, who got on the lifeboat in her place and ultimately survived.

In the Hollywood film, the two are shown in their chambers, embracing each other in bed as water fills compartment after compartment, sloshing beneath their mattress. According to many sources, however, they were last seen sitting next to each other on the deck of the ship, holding hands as the last lifeboats departed, before the ship itself halved and pitched, sinking slowly into the icy waters of the North Atlantic.

It is a sad story, but Jews have a keen sense of tragedy, and the honor and pride that can often be found within. The Jewish community, my parents included, would retell the story of these two Jews who were brave and loyal and honorable in the face of certain death. Years later, I hired an aide on my campaign staff named Jessica Straus. A few weeks after we hired her, I asked, almost offhand, if she was related to the Strauses who were on the *Titanic*. "Yes," she said. "I'm Isidor and Ida's great-great-granddaughter." Even when you don't expect it, Jewish history is all around you.

Why did that story matter to my parents? Why was Sandy Koufax taking a day off so inspirational? In part, it was because only a few Jews were appointed to positions of power in America during the first half of the twentieth century. Louis Brandeis, Benjamin Cardozo, and Felix Frankfurter were on the Supreme Court. Oscar Straus (a brother of Isidor Straus) was the Secretary of Commerce and Labor for President Teddy Roosevelt; Henry Morgenthau Jr. served as Secretary of Treasury in the FDR and Truman administrations. In New York, Herbert Lehman was elected governor. Jews were always aware of who was the first Jewish *this* or the first Jewish *that*. But they were few and far between at the time. So we cherished our boxers and baseball players, musicians and writers, labor activists and suffragettes, intellectuals and philanthropists, our geniuses (Einstein) and comedians (Marx Brothers), and one devoted elderly couple. We held them close and considered their triumphs and tribulations our own.

The stories of Jewish heroes were special, in part, because they showed that Jews had contributed so much to America at a time when many well-known, respected, and powerful people were trying to denigrate Jewish contributions. Henry Ford, Ambassador Joseph Kennedy, and Charles Lindbergh were ardent antisemites and made no effort to hide their hatred of the Jews; Walt Disney was known for inviting the Nazi film director Leni Riefenstahl to his studios in 1938. While it was common to say about someone, "They're Jewish" or "They're not Jewish," every so often you would say, "They're an antisemite." You knew which businesses, both local and national, did not hire Jews. You knew which associations and organizations refused to accept Jews, which hospitals and law firms did not hire Jewish doctors or lawyers.

These were the hallmarks of a tribe: shared heroes and villains and a distinct cultural mythology. More than that, though, there was a real sense of group identity. We believed that we'd rise and fall together. We looked out at the world through the same prism, a lens we were born with. If something happened in the world, a major event or even a minor occurrence, my parents would wonder aloud, "Is it good for the Jews?" If the stock market went up, was that good for the Jews? If so-and-so won the election, was it good for the Jews? If the Yankees beat the Red Sox, was it good for the Jews? It wasn't that we didn't consider ourselves Americans, New Yorkers, or Bostonians. In fact, we were extremely proud to be Americans. It was only that being Jewish added a different dimension to our impression of the world. Our people's history had created in Jews a collective consciousness. Deep down, we felt, the world could always turn against us. That question—Was it good for the Jews?—was always half-serious, half-not.

My own relationship with Judaism, the religion, was an evolving one, much as it was for generations of Schumers. My great-grandfather, for example, lived in a small town in Eastern Europe called Chortkiv. He was a devoutly religious man and a scholar of some renown in the area. Like most Jews in the region, who had severe restrictions placed on where they could work and where they could travel, my great-grandfather was poor. So my grandfather Jacob (or Jack) was sent across the Atlantic at a very young age, without an education or a penny to his name. He and his three youngest siblings were sent to live with an uncle-in-law in America, but the uncle turned out to be a ne'er-do-well, so my grandfather wound up a street urchin, sleeping in doorways, stealing apples off pushcarts to survive. One day when it was pouring rain, he saw a large number of people going into a building. They weren't charging admission, so he thought, *Let me go in and get dry.* That moment proved to be influential in his, and eventually my, life. Jews call it "bashert"—destiny, or God's hand.

The building was the Labor Temple on the Lower East Side, built by the unions to teach poor immigrants about the labor movement. The speakers that day happened to be Will Durant and Eugene V. Debs, famous leaders of the labor movement and among the greatest orators of their day. My grandfather was entranced and stayed for six hours. It was his first major intellectual experience. That was the day he became a union guy. Eventually he wound up in Utica, New York, working in a tissue-making factory called Doeskin and proselytizing for people to join the paper workers union. He lost his job during the Second World War, so he came back to New York City, where he bought a small exterminating business from a German-American who

12

was so sure the Nazis were going to bomb New York that he was fleeing to Montana. The religion of Judaism never meant all that much to my grandfather—he proclaimed that he was an agnostic—but he was a proudly Jewish person. Even though he didn't study the Torah or Talmud like his father before him, he was a quiet intellectual in a sense. He would tell me that he read Spinoza, the great Jewish philosopher who personally discarded the religion but believed that God was everywhere and in everything.

My grandfather, out of a lack of religious conviction, didn't Bar Mitzvah my father, a fact my father was often embarrassed about. As far as he knew, he was the only Jewish kid in his Utica neighborhood who didn't have one. While my father always felt a touch self-conscious, he considered himself as Jewish as his friends who were Bar Mitzvahed, and he understood that he was seen as Jewish by everyone else. Being Jewish and being seen as Jewish didn't require going through all the ceremonies, a lesson that was reinforced when my father was in grade school. The non-Jewish kids bullied the Jewish kids regularly. My father is the oldest of three, by five and six-and-a-half years, and had to defend his little brothers, Harry and Shelley. It didn't matter so much on the playground if you were technically Bar Mitzvahed or not.

My mother was a little bit more religious than my father, but our family's Jewishness wasn't grounded in religion. We'd go to synagogue on the High Holy Days, Rosh Hashanah and Yom Kippur, the two biggest holidays of the Jewish calendar, but we weren't going to services every Saturday. We'd have dinner every Friday night at home, when Jews typically mark the start of the Sabbath, but we never called it Shabbat dinner. It was Friday Night Dinner. My grandparents on both sides would come over, sometimes my uncles and aunts, too. My mother would make chicken and we'd have a boxed cake from Ebinger's, a German bakery. Even though Ebinger's wouldn't employ Jews, Blacks, or Latinos at the time, we decided the cake was too good. Over coffee and Ebinger's famous black-out cake, we'd argue with each other about everything. It was like the secular American version of the Talmudic debates that must have dominated Shabbat dinners in the Old World, where my great-grandfather held court. Who's going to win the election? The pennant? Which deli has the best pastrami? It was argument for argument's sake; how my family expressed its love and joy at being together. For me, Judaism was not a formal training; it was discussion and debate. It was food and it was family.

Still, my father insisted that my brother and I would have Bar Mitzvahs. And to get a Bar Mitzvah, you had to go to a Hebrew school. Its sole purpose in those days was not to teach you about Judaism or to immerse you in the Hebrew language, it was to get young boys through the ceremony. I studied Hebrew the way most Reform Jews studied it. We learned the phonetics of the language—because you needed to read and memorize Hebrew to recite your Torah portion, the essential task of the Bar Mitzvah—but not the meaning of the words. To this day, I can read Hebrew, but I have no earthly idea what it means. Part of being Jewish is not always knowing what everything means.

Our temple was a big Reform synagogue, a less orthodox type of Judaism, with a well-known but not well-liked rabbi named Rabbi Steinbach. He was a scholar and an orator of some repute who used to take on the affectation of an Old Testament scold.

"Oh, God has given you a good book. Forsake it not!" he intoned. The congregation rolled its eyes.

Despite his rhetorical fire-and-brimstone, Rabbi Steinbach wasn't a particularly strict follower of the commandments. When our more religious relatives came to visit, they were shocked by how he concluded his Sabbath sermons. He would invite the congregation to leave money in the tzedakah (charity) box, which is verboten—forbidden—by the Orthodox, who do not handle money on the Sabbath, when services are held. This breaking of the rules was a shanda, a shame or disgrace. My relatives murmured their disapproval.

In my youth, the big decision before everyone's Bar Mitzvah was whether to have a party during the day or at night, the latter of which was more expensive. As a kid, I was cheap, and still am, an unfortunate confirmation of that particular Jewish stereotype. I was always worried my father didn't have enough money. I'd heard him pacing the floors at 3 a.m. on Sunday nights, dreading the week ahead, wondering if he would be able to make ends meet. There wasn't much of a discussion. We settled on a day party.

The day before my Bar Mitzvah, I was in class at Cunningham Junior High School, when my English teacher, Mr. Zwerling, stopped the class and told everyone that he had an announcement. Mr. Zwerling was an old codger, the kind of rumpled suit that kids from time immemorial have distrusted and found impossible to relate to. No one believed him when he told us President John F. Kennedy had been shot. At the end of class, everyone filed out into the hallway and saw our classmates huddled together, crying by their lockers. Only then did we believe old Mr. Zwerling.

I went home that evening and our family was in a panic. We were shocked by the news, but just as urgently—or so it felt in the moment—we had to decide whether to hold my Bar Mitzvah party barely twenty-four hours after the president was assassinated. As we debated, my mother's brother, Uncle Morty (the only doctor in the family, so what he said was gospel), reasoned that we should not let a tragedy, even one as great as this, stop us from going forward with this Bar Mitzvah, always an important milestone in a Jewish boy's life. So we decided to go through with it.

A Bar Mitzvah is already a nerve-racking moment for a young man. You're thirteen years old, in the throes of puberty and crippling self-consciousness. You must stand in front of all your friends and family and chant long passages, from memory, in an ancient language that you can only barely read. On a normal weekend there would be a hundred, maybe two hundred people at our synagogue, a respectable but manageable number for an adolescent performer. But this Saturday was different from all other Saturdays. There wasn't an empty seat in the house. The entire neighborhood had come to mourn Kennedy. It was packed to the rafters. I was so nervous, I screwed up my Torah portion—Vayetze, Jacob's ladder—fumbling over words I didn't understand. To make matters worse, there was a pall over everything, including the party. It was terrible.

By the time dinner was served, everyone wanted to go home. I still remember my father—my lovely, sweet, decent father, who struggled to pay for the Bar Mitzvah—arguing with the caterer, a man named Yerna Kaufman, because he didn't serve after-dinner drinks and we had paid for them, seventy-five cents per person. Some have described Judaism as an ongoing argument with God. But my experience as a thirteen-year-old taught me that it also involved arguing with a lot of other Jews over trivialities. On the day that was supposed to be my graduation to a new and more adult connection to my faith, I, instead, felt just about finished with religion.

Later in life, my relationship with religion evolved. I was elected to the New York State Assembly in 1974. When you are in the assembly, most of the politics is performed at the local level: at parades and fairgrounds, graduations and little leagues. Some of the most important places to visit were houses of worship because that was where people gathered. Their leaders were pillars of their communities. My assembly district had a growing Orthodox population, and I started to visit more of the Orthodox temples. I found that I really enjoyed them—the spirituality, the rootedness, the rules, and the rhythm. The most modern Orthodox movement was called Young Israel, and I got to know some of their rabbis. They were not so extreme that they wanted to remove themselves from society. They had one foot in the dynamic, modern, secular world, and one foot planted in a world deeply rooted in ancient wisdom, where the practices and expressions revolved, like orbits, around the gravitational force of religious tradition. It seemed to me a wonderful combination, a way to give people a sense of responsibility but also a sense of belonging. I started to have more admiration for religion and its importance in a modern world. When I got married, I'd asked the rabbi I liked best, Rabbi Solomon Sharfman, from an Orthodox synagogue called Young Israel of Flatbush, to perform the ceremony.

After I was elected a US senator in 1998, I started to visit a much broader range of religious institutions: Catholic and

Protestant churches throughout the state of New York, as well as mosques, Sikh temples, and the Baptist churches around New York City. Just as when I was an assemblyman, I discovered that these were places where people found meaning, connection, and grounding in their lives. Oddly enough, I found my way back to the Jewish religion in part by visiting Christian congregations and swaying along to the gospel hymns at the Bridge Street AME on Easter.

For me, someone who believes deeply in God but doesn't follow the strict letter of biblical law, my respect for the Jewish religion deepened my connection to Jewish culture and history. Without the Jewish religion, would the Jewish culture and history have evolved the way that it did? I'm not sure it would have, or that you can completely separate one from the other. And so, like my father before me, I felt it was important to pass some of the religion down to my children. I had my daughters Bat Mitzvahed, and sent them to Hebrew school, where they had a much more engaging experience than I had had. My daughter Jessica had her Bat Mitzvah in Israel, on the arid plateau of Masada, where a besieged group of ancient Jews held out for weeks against the Romans before choosing to take their own lives rather than convert and become subjects of the Roman Empire. You can see why it became a symbol for the nascent state of Israel. Israeli Jews, too, have a keen sense of tragedy, and the pride and honor that can be found within.

WHEN I THINK back on my childhood and my family, I have never really questioned what made us Jewish. It was in the ether, the community, the bloodstream. Whether we were comfortable with the label or not, or thought of ourselves as more or less Jewish than other families, the world considered us Jewish. There was no deciding. We just were—the way Tony Tarricone was Italian and his wife Mary was Irish.

I also knew that my family's Jewishness was not the only model. My great-grandfather and my great-uncles and great-aunts were more religious; my grandfather, on the other hand, felt the divine spirit when he was fighting for working people. One of the great ironies of his career as a businessman was that, as the owner of a small exterminating company, he encouraged his own two employees to join a union and bargain collectively against him.

Our Jewishness wasn't about where we came from, either. We had Jewish relatives and friends from Poland and Russia, and our family who stayed behind in Europe was from the part of Galicia that is in present-day Ukraine. My Jewish friends' families were from all over Europe: France and Germany and Hungary and Czechoslovakia. A few were from Jewish families who had previously lived in China. I didn't know many Israeli Jews at the time, but I would come to as I got older.

What binds Jews together is not religion or geographic origin or even any specific group of beliefs. There are Central and Eastern European Jews, the Ashkenazi; Spanish, Portuguese, and Southern European Jews, the Sephardim; and Middle Eastern and North African Jews, the Mizrahi; as well as Jews from plenty of other places besides. There are Ethiopian Jews and African-American Jews and Amazonian Jews. There are Ultra-Orthodox Jews, Orthodox Jews, Conservative Jews, and Reform Jews, as well as agnostic and atheist Jews. (There are even Jews for Jesus, confusingly.) There are Jews who segregate themselves from modern society, the Hasidim and Haredim, religious fundamentalists whose customs are as strange to secular Jews as they might be to anyone else. There are socialist Jews, living in small farming communities in Israel called kibbutzim and raising their children communally, and there are capitalist Jews, who tend to draw the ire of your garden-variety antisemite. There are Jews who vehemently defend Israel and, as proud Zionists, feel a deep passion for our ancestral homeland. And there are some Jews who vehemently criticize Israel and call themselves anti-Zionist. Jews may not be a large number, but we contain multitudes.

There's an old Jewish yarn that if you walk into a room with two Jews, there will be three opinions. Another old Jewish joke finds a man, Chaim, marooned on an island for twenty years before people discover his location. As the rescuers approach the island in their rowboat, they see three structures. When they arrive on the beach they say, "Chaim, you've been here twenty years alone, what are these buildings for?"

"The first is my house," says Chaim. "I've lived there for twenty years. The second is my synagogue. I've prayed there every day for the last twenty years, too."

"So what's the third structure?" the rescuers ask.

"Oh," says Chaim, "that's the synagogue I wouldn't set foot in for the past twenty years."

Sure, the punchlines are about how Jews like to disagree. But running through these old jokes and stories is another idea: that there is always a bit more to being Jewish than you might expect. Whenever you think there's two, there's really three.

What binds us all together is something more foundational

than opinions or even religious beliefs: our heritage. Jews are a nation of people. There is a collective kinship even if it's difficult to pin down precisely. The closest I can come to explaining it is the feeling you have when you meet a Jewish person from a vastly different part of the world. If you are a French Jew and you meet an Iranian Jew on a train, for example, you feel some kind of bond, or link—a sense of immediate and ineffable connection, born of shared experiences in how you were brought up, a shared history, and how you were treated by the world around you. Being Jewish is something bequeathed to you, a human and historical legacy to be embraced, denied, or avoided, but something that can never be erased.

WHY IS IT so important to understand what it means to be Jewish to understand and fight antisemitism? One reason is very simple. If you want to understand a form of hatred, it helps to understand the truth about the people who are hated, and how wrong the prejudices are. I also believe that understanding the complexity of the Jewish experience reduces confusion over the nature of antisemitism, which is sometimes coded as a religious argument or a historical phenomenon rather than a hatred—a form of prejudice that is as dangerous to Jews in our time as it was in the past.

Finally, understanding the multifaceted nature of Jewishness is important to overcoming antisemitism. If everyone learned a little bit more about what it means to be Jewish—its history, its meaning, its culture, and its ways—I believe the world would be less likely to engage in antisemitism and would be less likely to downplay or ignore its significance. Antisemitism, as a concept, is the exact opposite of Jewishness. The Jewish story is complex, varied, beautiful, and distinct. Antisemitism is not only evil and vicious, but simplistic. The better one understands the richness of the Jewish experience, the less likely one is to be antisemitic.

CHAPTER 3

ANTISEMITISM
THROUGHOUT HISTORY

In the long sweep of human civilization, antisemitism is closer to the norm in many societies, rather than the exception. Most of the city-states, empires, kingdoms, sultanates, dictatorships, and yes, democracies that Jews have ever lived in have at one time or another treated us with scorn, deprived us of rights, restricted our movements and ambitions, and condoned violence against us.

We need to understand how the cycle of antisemitism operates, this long recurring arc of persecution in Jewish history. It is the history of a people who may be accepted into a nation for a time; to build communities and assimilate (or not); allowed, even, to accumulate power and earn renown. But ultimately, these turn out to be fleeting eras, golden ages destined to fade, replaced by regimes and societies that turn against the

Jews and, by expulsion, conversion, or genocide, attempt to eliminate their presence.

From ancient Egypt, Babylon, Greece, and Rome; to England, France, and Spain in the Middle Ages; to nineteenth-century Russia and twentieth-century Germany, this story has been repeated over and over and over again. It's a story that begins with hope and ends with trauma. Peaceful coexistence gives way to rising antisemitism, followed inevitably by violence against Jews. In the modern era, this cycle of tolerance, revulsion, and hatred culminated in the Holocaust—the industrial slaughter of more than six million Jews—a historical fact that Jews are still being asked by some to document and prove. The generations of Jews and non-Jewish allies who were born in the years after the Holocaust were taught to tell the world: "Never again." Jews are also trained to ask themselves: "Could it happen again?"

To JEWS, THE historical cycle of antisemitism is well known, the foundation of our greatest stories, the impulse behind our most important holidays. Our history is wrapped up in our holidays, and they are essential to understanding how Jews grow up learning about our place in the world. While other religions celebrate saviors and martyrs, saints and holy virtues, Jews celebrate two millennia of close shaves. The Haggadah, the sacred text of the Passover seder, commands us each year to recite: "In every generation, our enemies rise up to destroy us."

The story of Passover begins with Joseph, son of a Jewish patriarch, who was befriended by the Pharaoh's courtiers after a series of misadventures and betrayals found him marooned in Egypt. Joseph's wisdom and skill in interpreting dreams greatly impressed the desert monarch, who appointed him governor of Egypt. For a time, Joseph and his tribe lived in Egypt in peace, and helped the kingdom become rich and bountiful. Joseph's early years in Egypt are a reminder of the fact that Jews are often found at first to be useful by those in power and permitted to coexist alongside other citizens—but only so long as the ruler sees the Jews as an asset to the regime. Eventually, Joseph passed away and a new Pharaoh came along with a different idea about the Jews: Ramses II. This Pharaoh felt threatened by the growing number of Jews in his kingdom. They were forced into bondage and he ordered that their firstborn sons be slain. Moses, our most famous prophet as the recipient of the Ten Commandments, was ferried in a basket down the Nile to spare his life. He was rescued, then grew up and reluctantly assumed the heavy burdens of leadership. After God visited plagues upon the Egyptians to convince Pharaoh to let the Jews go, Moses led his people into both freedom and exile, parting the sea as they left Egypt.

Even a thousand years after their Exodus from Egypt, Jews were still being villainized in the region. Egypt in the third century BC was part of a sprawling empire that Alexander the Great's conquests had created, fusing disparate cultures and religions, and ushering in the Hellenistic era. During this period, an Egyptian priest called Manetho who was fluent in Greek recast the biblical chapter of the Exodus from a story of Jewish liberation to a story of Jewish expulsion from Egypt. In Manetho's telling, the Jews were driven from Egypt by a Pharaoh who believed he could communicate with the gods only if he "purified" his country of "unclean people." A few hundred years after Manetho, an Egypt-born Greek scholar named

Apion recycled many of Manetho's claims in the Roman Empire that Jews descended from a leprous group of Egyptian slaves and performed human sacrifices. Apion's slanders were strongly associated with stoking the growing antisemitism in the Roman and Greek world, and in 38 AD, the first pogrom against Jews was unleashed, in Alexandria.

A similar cycle of antisemitism appears in the story of Hanukkah. It begins with Alexander the Great, whose conquest of the biblical land of Canaan did not result in an immediate change of fate for the Jews living there. Under Alexander, the Jews were allowed to continue their customs and religious practices. But he died young, and his empire disintegrated. After his death, a new king came along, Antiochus IV, who cracked down on the Jews, outlawed their religious practice, and desecrated the Temple of Jerusalem, our holiest site, smearing it with pig's blood. A group of rebel Jews fled to the hills. Led by a family of guerrilla fighters, the Maccabees, they took back the Temple and rededicated it to its sacred purpose. The bit that most people remember about holy oil miraculously burning for eight days is more like a footnote to a story about Jews fighting for their lives in present-day Israel.

Purim, a lesser-known holiday outside the Jewish faith, follows a similar pattern. The Book of Esther in the Bible recounts a portion of the history of the Jews in Persia, living under King Ahasuerus, who marries a young Jewish woman, Esther, who hid her ancestry, as many Jews did and would continue to do for centuries. The king's top advisor, Haman, becomes jealous of a Jewish man at court named Mordecai—who had uncovered an assassination plot against the king and was bestowed honors for his loyalty—and conspires to exterminate the Jews in the kingdom. He casts "lots" to determine the date of the massacre. When Mordecai tells Esther of this plan, she reveals her identity to the king and convinces him to spare the Jews. At synagogues all over the world, this drama is reenacted every year with theatrical performances, usually in the form of a spoof—called a spiel, a Yiddish derivative now widely used in the English-speaking world. Purim, which means "lots," is a celebration of the Jews' narrow escape from a planned genocide.

As the joke goes, you can sum up every Jewish holiday in three phrases: "They tried to kill us. We survived. Let's eat."

It's safe to say that Christian holidays have a very different vibe. In most Christian celebrations, there is a sense of uplift. Even tragic commemorations, like the Passion and the crucifixion (because of course, early Christians did experience significant persecution), tend to end on a note of grace or wonder. The anticipation of Easter is the resurrection of Christ, and the absolution of mankind from sin. The conclusion of most Jewish holidays is a sigh of relief—we escaped—and a polite reminder to try to relive the pain our people went through. It has instilled in Jews a heightened sense of danger; the presumption that small worries turn into large problems. We are attuned, by rite, to be aware of the precariousness of the Jew's place in society, how abruptly things might turn. My non-Jewish friends don't always grasp the intensity of that feeling, and I think that contributes to the tendency of some people to believe that Jews overreact to antisemitism.

I worry sometimes, too, about overreacting. There is a natural fear of not wanting to cry wolf. But when I look out at the world, I see that targeting Jewish temples, the basis of Hanukkah, which took place in the second century before Christ, remains a strategy for antisemites in the twenty-first century after Christ. The Temple in Jerusalem and the Tree of Life synagogue in Pittsburgh suffered a similar fate; their floors were smeared with Jewish blood. The idea that Jews are connected to pestilence or plague, an aspect of the Passover story, inspired antisemites across medieval Europe and Nazi Germany, and has found expression again in Covid-era conspiracy theories. The Nazis planned the murders of Jews to coincide with Purim. For many Jews, our holidays do not feel like a reminder of our history; they feel like a warning about the future.

We feel a generational burden to impart the warning to our descendants. I am blessed with two beautiful daughters, Alison and Jessica. Whenever our family traveled in Europe, we made it a point to investigate the Jewish history of the area. The Jewish quarter of Prague. The Jewish ghettos in Rome and Venice. The memorial to the deportation of the Jews in Paris. Even on holiday, Jewish tragedy is never far from sight. And while these were not joyous excursions, my wife, Iris, and I felt that they were important places to show our daughters. That I felt compelled, as a young father, to take my daughters to these places taught me something about my own attachment to my Jewish identity.

Now we are blessed with three young grandchildren: Noah and Ellie, by my daughter Jessica and her husband, Michael; and Henry, by my daughter Alison and daughter-in-law Elizabeth. Last year, we celebrated Purim together as a family. Noah is now old enough to understand the stories you tell him, while Ellie and Henry are still too young. As my son-in-law was retelling the story of Purim to Noah, we decided to stop him before the end. We weren't ready to tell my sweet little grandson, just yet, that Haman wanted to murder the Jews. We thought he'd be scared, and we knew there would come a time, soon, when we would have to tell him that there are people in the world who want to kill the Jews. Sometimes I worry that the world will reveal that truth to him first, before we get the chance to warn him.

JEWISH HOLIDAYS DRAW from our experience in the ancient world, but there are plenty of examples of antisemitism running its full course through societies in every era. David Nirenberg's well-regarded history on this subject, *Anti-Judaism: The Western Tradition*, traces the recurring cycle across twenty-three centuries. Paul Johnson's *A History of the Jews* and Simon Schama's *The Story of the Jews* contain many of the same themes. Examples abound. There are some historical chapters known to many, like the stories of the Jewish holidays. There are some that occurred later that are less widely known. In England, thousands of Jews lived mostly in peace alongside Christians before Edward I expelled them in 1290. With his kingdom in debt, the king seized Jewish property and transferred debts owed to the Jews to the Crown, before marching the exiles to the southern coast and forcing them across the channel. In medieval Spain, Jews, Christians, and Muslims lived in relative harmony for hundreds of years—a period called the *Convivencia*, the "living together"—before the forced conversion and expulsion of the Jews during the Catholic reunification of Spain in 1492 and the Inquisition that followed. In fact, recent scholarship has uncovered that converted Jews, known as Conversos or Marranos, were likely responsible for financing the voyage of Christopher Columbus to the New World in 1492. A study by Spanish geneticists based on two decades of research into the heritage of Columbus revealed an even more intriguing possibility: that Columbus himself was a Sephardic Jew who concealed his Jewish identity or converted to Christianity. Even today, people are still discovering the many ways in which Jews and antisemitism have shaped the history of the modern world.

The Jewish ghettos and quarters my family and I visited in Europe were geographic markers to this history, places where Jews might have thrived and greatly influenced the course of their societies, but which eventually and inevitably became ghost towns. What led to all these haunted houses? What tools did leaders use to turn their societies against the Jews? What ideas about Jews have persisted across centuries, fueling and shaping antisemitism? Which prejudices still exist today?

Just like antisemitism has a pattern in history, there's a pattern to how it manifests in cultures across the world. It can range from relatively harmless stereotypes to more pernicious tropes. On the more superficial side of things: having curly hair, a prominent schnoz, or being stingy. And why do Jews have such big noses? As one old insult goes, because air is free. Being "Jewish" can be pejoratively interpreted to mean litigious, opinionated, argumentative, or whiney; shifty, sneaky, untrustworthy, a cheat; book smart but bad at sports; weak or sniveling; a lawyer or an accountant. The greedy and vengeful Shylock, the most prominent Jewish character in Shakespeare, demands a "pound of flesh" from Antonio in *The Merchant of Venice* as payment for a defaulted loan. In European literature, the Jewish protagonist was often portrayed as cunning, shrewd, amoral, and parsimonious. In English slang, you can be "jewed down" on the price of something or "jewed out" of something you are entitled to.

These ideas are widespread, and the vast majority of non-Jews will have heard at least one of these stereotypes, and likely many more. Jews will have heard their non-Jewish friends, even by accident and without spite, refer to one of them in passing.

In the dogma of antisemitism, Jews are not to be trusted and are always out for themselves. We are cast as a fifth column, engaged in espionage against, or sabotage of, our home nations. In ancient times, leaders seized on the idea that the Jewish minority living in their civilization was working against the regime, undermining it or poisoning it from within. In modern times, it is much the same. In America, the presence of Jews in leadership positions in the Communist Party and other left-wing organizations was used to paint all Jews as radical activists. Jews have long been suspected and accused of dual loyalty: that our true allegiance is with the Jewish state of Israel instead of whichever country we actually live in.

Another common manifestation of antisemitism was plain discrimination: societies creating one set of formal or informal rules for non-Jews, and a different set of rules for Jews. One of the earliest forms of antisemitism in Europe—dating back to the Middle Ages—were strict legal codes that prevented Jews from participating fully in society. Jews could not freely live in the cities, only in rural areas, or ghettos or segregated quarters within cities. Jews were not allowed to join guilds and be craftsmen, or own land and be farmers. For a while, Jews could not visit or live in Moscow. The reason that many Jews turned to money lending in these societies was because they were prohibited from nearly every other profession, and because Christians considered usury—charging interest on loans to fellow Christians—a sin. Unsurprisingly, Jews would come to be hated for that, too. In recent decades, there might not have been such overt, institutionalized discrimination against Jews but a double standard still exists, as seen in the way much of the world treats Israel differently than any other nation, a topic I'll cover later in some depth.

Throughout history, Jews have often been the scapegoat of choice for the ills of the world. One of the most enduring antisemitic tropes is the accusation that the Jews were and remain collectively responsible for the death of Jesus Christ, even though he was crucified by the Romans. It is a canard that you still hear today, more than two thousand years since the events in question.

In the Middle Ages, Jews were blamed for deliberately spreading the bubonic plague by poisoning drinking wells. The reason? Jewish religious traditions like handwashing and storing grain outdoors (which limited the number of rats in Jewish dwellings) meant that fewer Jews died from the plague than most other peoples. So of course, the Jews were suspect. In the aftermath of the First World War, Germany suffered a lost economic decade—a result of losing the war and the punishing terms of the Treaty of Versailles. Adolf Hitler and the Nazi Party blamed Germany's impoverished state on "international finance Jewry," and it wasn't long before they were using the lexicon of parasites and vermin when referring to the Jews of Europe.

When something starts to go rotten in the state of affairs, Jews are often the first to get the blame. You don't have to plumb the depths of the internet to find sites and forums dedicated to blaming Jews for the financial crisis, 9/11, and more. Robert F. Kennedy Jr., a devoted conspiracy theorist and erstwhile candidate for president and, as I write, nominee for Secretary of the Department of Health and Human Services, speculated that Covid was engineered to spare Ashkenazi Jews.

A related idea is that Jews are behind the scenes controlling and benefiting from systems of power. Recall the conspiracy theories that Jews run the media, Hollywood, and the international banking system; or secretly orchestrate world affairs, that the Rothschilds and George Soros wield immense power over geopolitics. The most extreme examples include claims that Jews were not in the Twin Towers on 9/11 because Mossad had warned them the attack was coming, or that Jews control the weather. A candidate for Congress—now a congresswoman—ventured a convoluted hypothesis on Facebook that a massive California wildfire had been sparked by a laser beam from space, fired by a utility connected to the Rothschilds—giving birth to the concept of "Jewish space lasers." The antisemite believes Jews are agitators and conspirators, the puppet masters pulling the strings. The prototypical example of this strain of antisemitism is the *Protocols of the Elders of Zion*, a deliberately fabricated text published in Imperial Russia in the early twentieth century that describes a Jewish plot for global domination. Henry Ford was so taken with the text, he had portions of its English translation published in a series of virulently antisemitic articles titled "The International Jew: The World's Problem" in his newspaper, the *Dearborn Independent*. Despite its spurious origins, the *Protocols* continues to be cited and read and shared and downloaded and believed well into the twenty-first century.

Antisemitic tropes about Jewish power and influence have endured. I believe they contribute to the tendency today to label

Jews and Israel as "oppressors," and to presume all Jews are white, even though a significant percentage of Jews worldwide are of Middle Eastern, Arab, or North African descent. In many ways, the idea that Jews control systems of power is one of the most painful and powerful strains of antisemitism, because it casts doubt on the validity of any success that the Jewish people have achieved, weaponizing it against them and pitting them against their fellow citizens. Not only does this idea feed directly into the tendency to scapegoat Jews for everything that goes wrong in a society, it also makes it harder for some people to believe that Jews can also be victims of bigotry and prejudice. Antisemitism, sometimes by design and sometimes by accident, reinforces itself.

REFLECTING ON THE long history of antisemitism leaves me with a lingering and unsettling question: Why were Jews reviled in so many eras and in so many parts of the world? We can guess at a few reasons. One might be that Judaism is the oldest monotheistic religion. The religions that came afterward, religions that would dominate Western societies and the Middle East, Africa, and Asia, had to express themselves in relation to Judaism. By definition, the new religions had to explain why the old religion was no longer good enough (as Judaism had to define itself against polytheism and idolatry). Part of the foundational narrative of Christianity and Islam is that Jews had gone astray or had the wrong idea about the nature of God and the moral universe. On the very extreme ends of those religions, Jews are considered infidels destined to burn in eternal hellfire.

Another reason might be that Jews have almost always been

a demographic minority and, absent a hundred years or so in biblical times, stateless. We were subject to the whims of more powerful tribes, rulers, and religions. Bullies tend to pick on the smallest kids on the playground, the ones who look, act, and pray differently. For similar reasons, antisemitism became a deliberate political strategy, a way to create cohesion among the majority population by giving them something and somebody to rally against. David Nirenberg makes the case that leaders would often define the virtues of their civilization or ideology by labeling opposite qualities as "Jewish." Because Jews were the minority and already seen as outsiders, it was easy for leaders to make the Jews out to be villains. The surest way to whip up fervor and hatred against a group is to say that they represent the very opposite of whatever you have been brought up to love, cherish, and value. The writer Dara Horn summarized his point in a February 2024 essay: "If piety was a given society's ideal, Jews were impious blasphemers; if secularism was the ideal, Jews were backward pietists. If capitalism was evil, Jews were capitalists; if communism was evil, Jews were communists. If nationalism was glorified, Jews were rootless cosmopolitans; if nationalism was vilified, Jews were chauvinistic national-ists." The historian Simon Schama references the influential Roman historian Tacitus, who wrote a slanderous account of Jewish history in Egypt and the Holy Land, as an exemplar of this particular strain of thought in the pagan world. According to the historian Erich Gruen, who translated the work of the Roman historian, Tacitus believed the Jews to be "a race of men hated by the gods. They regard as profane everything that we (Romans) hold as sacred—and vice versa. Their practices are base and wicked, and prevail through their own depravity....

Those who cross over to their ways scorn the gods, abandon their own nation, and hold their parents, siblings, and children cheap. Jewish rites are sordid and ridiculous. Jews throughout their history were the most despised of subject peoples and the basest of nations."

Nirenberg's most powerful argument is that anti-Jewish sentiment is based on more than two thousand years of non-Jewish people thinking about Jews and how they're different from them, not only religiously but across many different dimensions. The Pharaohs, the early Christians, and Muslims had to formulate how they were different from the Jews to make sense of the cosmos. And as societies in the Middle Ages developed new forms of poetry, philosophy, and politics, people thought about those topics in relation to how Jews living in their societies thought about them. Medieval and early modern people, Nirenberg writes, "imagined their critical task as Christian or Muslim worshippers, as artists, writers, philosophers, as citizens and politicians, to be the identification and overcoming of the threat of Judaism within their ranks." Over and over again, many people constructed their conception of the world in relation to Judaism and Jews, defining themselves in some manner of opposition to the Jewish religion, culture, and people. This work is still going on.

Antisemitism is a very old idea, well established, with an intellectual history and a language. There's a rubric for hating Jews, for distrusting them, for blaming them for your problems or your country's problems. It's a tactic that's been shown to work, and it has been well practiced by pharaohs and kings, dictators and demagogues. Antisemitism is always right there in case you need it. Far from being merely an element of Western thought and culture, antisemitism and a reaction to Jews has helped shape them. Jean-Paul Sartre's famous argument bears repeating: "If the Jew did not exist, the anti-Semite would invent him."

There are, however, certain conditions, technologies, and political ideas that make it more likely for leaders or societies to latch on to antisemitism. We will explore them in this book, especially those factors that are driving antisemitism today. But even when a society appears healthy, tolerant, and inclusive, history teaches us that it is not because antisemitism has been permanently defeated, but rather because it is lying dormant for a time.

JEWS LEARN ABOUT the cycle of antisemitism from our holidays and history, and we celebrate stories of rebellion, persecution, and survival—moments when Jews triumphed over great adversity, narrowly avoiding a terrible fate at the last possible moment. But the truth about antisemitism is that, unlike our holidays, all too often the Jewish people do not escape by the collective skins of our teeth. Instead, the Jews suffer some great calamity.

Working backward, one can trace a long line through history of our greatest traumas: October 7, 2023, in Southern Israel; 2018 at the Tree of Life synagogue in Pittsburgh; 1999 at the Los Angeles Jewish Community Center; 1986 at Neve Shalom Synagogue in Istanbul; 1974 at Netev Meir Elementary School in Ma'alot; the 1973 Yom Kippur War in the Sinai Peninsula and Golan Heights; 1972 at the Munich Olympics and Lod Airport; the 1930s and '40s in Germany and Central Europe; the 1880s to 1900s in the Pale of Settlement; 1679 in Yemen; 1492 in Spain; 1394 in France; 1290 in England; during the Crusades in the Middle Ages; 629 in Galilee; 70 in Jerusalem; 586 BC in Judea; 722 BC in Samaria; the thirteenth century BC in Egypt. For millennia, the Jewish people have been humiliated, ostracized, expelled, enslaved, and massacred. This list includes merely the most memorable flashpoints of expulsion, terrorism, or mass violence against Jews. For Jews who lived through these eras, antisemitism was likely a condition of daily life.

At least in modern times, when the cycle of antisemitism reached its final stages, and mass violence was perpetrated against the Jews, humanity recoiled. This is how the cycle resets itself. The Holocaust lifted the veil, and this was the precursor to the longest period of safety for Jews in America and in Israel. The world was so shocked by what happened that it was resolved that antisemitism must be kept in check, and for the first time in modern history, world powers endorsed the concept and creation of a Jewish nation-state. As Justice Robert H. Jackson said at the opening of the Nuremberg trials, "The wrongs which we seek to condemn and punish have been so calculated, so malignant, and so devastating, that civilization cannot tolerate their being ignored, because it cannot survive their being repeated." Civilization did not ignore or condone those crimes, at least for a time.

Our responsibility today is to break the cycle of antisemitism before it reaches a more devastating phase—to identify and fight antisemitism when it starts to bubble up, but before it boils over. When Jews see rising antisemitism, our instinct is to fear what might come next, and our every impulse is to shout from the ramparts for others to join us in stopping it, because history has also taught us that Jews, alone, cannot protect themselves. The goal of every modern society, and every decent person, should be to avoid another repetition of the cycle.

CHAPTER 4

ANTISEMITISM IN AMERICA

How bad could antisemitism get in America, given its virulent history in the world?

In the 1950s, fifty years after my grandfather immigrated to the United States, and not long after the full extent of the Holocaust had been revealed to the world, he told me that he had actually rooted for Germany over Russia in World War I. As a child, he'd heard that the Germans treated the Jewish people much better than the Russians, who he knew to be virulently antisemitic. Imperial Russia had designated territory within the western region of its growing empire as the Pale of Settlement, in which Jews could live, but outside of which Jews were forbidden to even travel for work. Even within the Pale of Settlement, Jews were barred from residing in a number of cities and were barred from many professions. There were waves of pogroms, from the 1880s to the early 1920s, encouraged or condoned by Russian governments. Marauding bands of Ukrainian peasants, Polish townsfolk, Russian soldiers, and in the deadliest wave that killed tens of thousands between 1919 and 1921, Cossacks—the mounted units of the Russian Volunteer Army—would sweep into Jewish villages and towns, set the houses on fire, beat the Jewish men, and sometimes rape Jewish women. (In fact, it is part of Jewish lore that if you have blond hair and blue eyes, some of your female ancestors might have had some unwanted Cossack DNA contributed to your family line.)

By contrast, in the early 1900s, German Jewry was one of the most secure and prosperous ethnic communities in Europe. It was also loyal. More than 100,000 German Jews served in World War I; around 12,000 died for their country. The Jewish community in Germany was among the most affluent in Europe, and German Jews achieved a level of prominence in business, science, literature, cinema, music, and theater. In fact, between 1880 and 1914, when more than 2 million Russian Jews fled with the intent to emigrate to America, some 80,000 of them chose to stay in Germany. At the time, Germany didn't seem so different from America when it came to its attitude toward Jews.

When the Nazis first marched in the streets and held rallies decrying the so-called international financiers, war profiteers, and communists, many Germans either stayed silent or marched alongside them, perhaps not realizing what they were aiding and abetting. But it was abundantly clear by the time Adolf Hitler took the podium at the Reichstag in January 1939 and described Jews as "parasite[s] living on the body and the productive work of other nations." The shattering violence of

Kristallnacht had occurred three months earlier, when across Germany, Jewish businesses and synagogues were burned to the ground, Jewish cemeteries desecrated, and tens of thousands of Jewish men arrested and sent to concentration camps.

Over time, Nazi rhetoric and the enactment of the Nuremberg laws—a series of racially discriminatory restrictions placed on all Jewish-German residents—had softened the ground for what Hitler stated at the Reichstag was his true and ultimate goal: "the annihilation of the Jewish race in Europe." Many of those Germans of goodwill, who marched in the early years of Hitler's ascension, chose to stay on the sidelines even after his horrifying intent was made clear. The result was the most systematic and largest genocide in human history. Six million Jewish people were exterminated in a few short years.

The farther we get from the Nazi era, the more confined it might feel to history. But we must remember that in the early twentieth century Germans overall were regarded as modern, educated, and prosperous. They were living in a highly cultured society, they had Jewish neighbors and relatives, and they shopped at Jewish businesses. Yet, in the span of a single decade, an opportunistic demagogue organized and inspired his country to condone or join his project of eliminating the Jewish population in Europe. And he nearly succeeded.

The relative recency of the Holocaust—more than two hundred thousand survivors are still alive today—and the depth of its horror forces Jews around the world, including in America, to wonder: *Could it happen again? Could it happen here?* Deep in our bones, we fear that, yes, it could happen again. I believe that was what my grandfather was trying to tell me. His experience had taught him that Jewish safety is a tenuous thing, even where it appears most secure. The unthinkable is, in fact, always possible.

AMERICA IS NO stranger to antisemitism. It has not existed here as deeply as it has in Europe, where it seems to grow in the soil, but America has undergone its own cycles of antisemitism: periods of outright exclusion and widespread discrimination, but also periods of relative acceptance and progress.

Jews have lived on the American continent since before our nation's founding. One of the earliest stories of Jewish immigration involves twenty-three Sephardic Jews who fled Brazil in 1654, after it had been retaken from the Dutch by the Portuguese, who expelled all Jews who did not convert to Catholicism. They would eventually land in New Amsterdam, the Dutch colony in present-day New York, where the director-general, Peter Stuyvesant, an avowed antisemite, firmly opposed their settlement. These twenty-three Sephardic emigrants asked fellow Jews in Amsterdam to petition the Dutch West India Company, which ran the colony, to allow their entry. The Dutch West India Company believed the Jewish people to be hardworking and an asset to the commercial future of the colony, and therefore told Stuyvesant to admit the Jewish refugees, who founded what is now the oldest Jewish congregation in the United States. Today, you will find cemeteries for Jews of Spanish and Portuguese descent in Lower Manhattan and Greenwich Village. Present in that early chapter of Jewish immigration are the kinds of reactions Jewish immigrants would face for hundreds of years in

America. On the one hand, obstinate antisemitism and rejection. On the other, a fair-minded tolerance, an openness to and an appreciation of their talents. That New York City always had an instinct for the latter, even in its early origins as a Dutch outpost, continues to make me proud.

A hundred and fifty years or so later, some of the Founding Fathers reflected a similar ambivalence toward Jews. While Thomas Jefferson was vocal in championing the rights of Jews to practice their faith like all other Americans, his private letters make clear that he held a decidedly negative view of Judaism, as did other Enlightenment rationalists of his generation. "Moses had bound the Jews," he wrote, "to many idle ceremonies, mummeries and observances, of no effect towards producing the social utilities which constitute the essence of virtue." John Adams, on the other hand, venerated ancient Jews for laying the groundwork for Christianity and wrote that the Jews "have influenced the affairs of mankind more, and more happily than any other nation, ancient or modern." George Washington's reflection on religious tolerance in America is perhaps the best remembered. Writing to a Rhode Island synagogue in 1790, Washington expressed a touching sentiment: "May the Children of the Stock of Abraham, who dwell in this land, continue to merit and enjoy the good will of the other Inhabitants; while everyone shall sit in safety under his own vine and fig tree, and there shall be none to make him afraid."

The Jewish community in America was small but steadily growing for the better part of our country's first century. There were a few notable figures and historical footnotes, including Judah P. Benjamin, a slaveholding senator from Louisiana, the second Jewish senator in American history, and the first not to renounce his faith. As the Secretary of War and then Secretary of State of the Confederacy, he practically served as the second-in-command to Jefferson Davis. The bulk of Jewish-Americans at the time lived in the North and supported the Union, but had the Confederacy won the Civil War, Judah P. Benjamin would have been the highest-ranking elected Jewish official in American history. Thankfully, the Union prevailed, and instead, that distinction belongs to the author.

German Jews began coming in large numbers to the United States in the middle of the nineteenth century, but the majority of Jewish-Americans arrived in the early part of the twentieth century. Between 1900 and 1924, 1.75 million Jews, mostly from Eastern Europe, arrived in the United States, nudging the Jewish share of the American population from 1 to 3.5 percent by 1930, a sizable shift that was more noticeable in East Coast cities, where Jews made up even higher percentages of the local population. That great mass of Jewish immigration, which includes many in my family, were well acquainted with antisemitism. Many were fleeing persecution and mob violence, including the pogroms. Many came to America in search of a better life and better economic prospects. Upon arriving, they found both opportunity and resistance, a country where they could live and raise their families without fear of organized violence, but also a country that was often uncomfortable with their presence.

In much the same way that the mass migration of the Irish, Italians, and Chinese to American shores in the mid-nineteenth century led to decades of intolerance, the mass migration of Jews provoked a reaction among native-born Americans. Signs that read NO IRISH NEED APPLY had new neighbors: GENTILES ONLY and NO DOGS OR JEWS ALLOWED. "Kike"—a slur for

Jews—entered the American lexicon at the turn of the century. Some hypothesized that it was because Jews signed their entry forms at Ellis Island with a circle instead of an X, which reminded them of the Christian cross ("kikel" is the Yiddish word for "circle"). The strain of antisemitism that Jewish immigrants encountered in America was less dangerous than its much older and angrier cousin in Europe, but it was nonetheless a culturally acceptable form of discrimination and was well established in America's corridors of power.

As you'd expect, anti-immigration sentiments in early-twentieth-century America reflected emerging themes about the undesirability of Jewish immigrants. Henry Cabot Lodge Sr., a blue-blooded Republican who was a massive figure in the US Senate at the time and considered the first Senate Majority Leader, was also the de facto spokesperson for the avowedly nativist Immigration Restriction League. While he spoke favorably of immigrants from Northern and Western Europe, he strenuously argued against admitting those from Southern and Eastern Europe, where most Jews were coming from. He once claimed, imperiously, that Jews "lack nobler abilities which enable a people to rule." Cabot Lodge would lead the fight in 1916 against the confirmation of Justice Brandeis to be the first Jewish justice on the Supreme Court and it wasn't long before these bigoted views were codified into law: The 1924 Johnson-Reed Act included severe quotas on immigrants from Eastern Europe, which effectively slowed Jewish immigration down to a trickle.

Most Jews of my generation grew up learning about the *St. Louis*, a passenger ship carrying 937 Jewish refugees fleeing the Third Reich in 1939. When the liner arrived in Havana, the Cuban government refused to let most of the passengers disembark, and soon forced it to leave. The *St. Louis* then sailed near the Florida coast, so close that passengers could see the flickering lights of Miami on the horizon. Newspapers across America reported the story with sympathy for the plight of the refugees. High-ranking officials in the State Department, and President Franklin Roosevelt's secretary of state, Tennessee's Cordell Hull, however, remained unmoved, refusing the refugees entry into the United States without proper immigration visas. Their indifference reflected the deep-seated antisemitism, xenophobia, and isolationist tendencies prevalent in America at the time. Not welcomed by Canada, either, the Jewish refugees were forced to return to Western Europe, with most of them being taken in by Great Britain, France, Belgium, and the Netherlands. A year later, Hitler's forces invaded Western Europe; 254 former passengers of the *St. Louis*, having been mere miles from sanctuary, were eventually killed during the Holocaust.

In America, among the powers that be, a degree of antisemitism was endemic, a viewpoint you could casually express at dinner parties or at the office without shame or fear of censure. In response, it wasn't uncommon for Jews to change their names or hide their religious identity, as Esther did in biblical times, to avoid institutional and societal discrimination. Jewish journalists would use initials to abbreviate their Semitic-sounding names; artists and performers would shorten or change their names entirely. I grew up reading bylines in the *New York Times* by "A.M. Rosenthal" instead of Abraham or Abe Rosenthal. Robert Zimmerman became Bob Dylan. One day, a kid in my second-grade class, Howard Finkelstein, came in after the Christmas break and told everyone that he was now Howard Fields; that kind of thing was not uncommon. The historian Kirsten Fermaglich estimates that in 1932, 65 percent of all name-change applications in New York City had Jewish-sounding surnames. For some, it was easier, and sometimes necessary, to shroud their Jewishness to win acceptance or approval of their peers—for many, to even get a job—a twentieth-century American version of an Old Testament phenomenon.

There's an old joke about a Jewish man who comes in front of a judge and says, "Your Honor, I want you should change my name."

"What's your name?" says the judge.

"My name is Isaac Rabinowitz."

"Well, Isaac, I can see why you want to change your name. What do you want to change it to?"

"Your Honor, I want you should change it to Henry Wilson Smith."

The judge does so, then bangs his gavel and calls up the next case.

Three months later, the same man comes before the judge. The judge says, "Isaac—sorry, I mean Henry—what brings you back?"

"Your Honor, I want you should change my name," he says.

"What do you mean? We just changed it three months ago! You're Henry Wilson Smith now."

"I know," says the man. "I want to be able to say I was Henry Smith before I changed my name."

Try as you might, you could never truly escape being Jewish.

As a young boy, I experienced a version of the blunt antisemitism that many Jews faced upon arriving in America. When I was eight years old, I was in a car with my father, mother, brother, and sister driving down Ocean Parkway in Brooklyn, on our way back home after a Friday Night Dinner at my grandparents' house. The driver of the car next to us rolled down his window at a stoplight and screamed at my father, "You fucking Jew," before speeding off. I can only imagine that he did it because we were in a particularly Jewish part of Brooklyn. My father told me not to let it bother me, but I could sense how much it had shaken him. That memory—the details of that small encounter—has stayed with me ever since, the feeling that some people thought that Jews would never belong here. At the time, I didn't understand what prompted the man, out of nowhere, to scream something so base and so vile to my nice father, who never hurt anybody. But I noticed that my father treated the incident as if it was not altogether unexpected. It was something to be played down, something to just get over with, like a rainy day or a traffic jam.

My friends growing up were mostly kids from the block around East Twenty-Seventh Street. They were Irish, Italian, and Jewish (we even called where we lived the neighborhood of the three *I*'s—Ireland, Italy, and Israel), and that was reflected in the makeup of the friends I had, a healthy mix of Catholic and Jewish kids. For the most part, everyone got along. But the monsignor at the local church was virulently antisemitic and often preached—descriptively—about how the Jews would go to hell because they killed Christ. We'd hear, from time to time, taunts, or insults, or just plain inquiries about being Jewish from our Catholic friends, things they heard at church or at home.

I remember one frigid winter day in Brooklyn, when we were still very young, some of the kids from the neighborhood told us, matter-of-factly, "You know, Jews go to hell."

We thought, *What's hell?*

Steam drifted up from the sewer grates as meltwater dripped on the hot pipes that ran underneath the city. One of the kids pointed and said, "It's down there. That's where the Jews are gonna go." And those were our friends!

Comments like those might have bothered us a little, but they weren't all that vicious and in fact were not meant to be vicious. In my family, the previous generations had had it so much worse. My father and uncles had recounted to me how they would get beaten up on the playground and when walking home from school in Utica, but I never experienced any such violence. Through my adolescence, antisemitism was something that you ran into but didn't live through on a daily basis. Like freezing water dripping over hot pipes, the reflexive intolerance experienced by my parents' and grandparents' generations was evaporating. Opportunities were being extended to Jews that had not been extended to them before. America was getting used to us, and Jews were getting used to living in America, building stronger and stronger communities. The rising number of Jewish families in the American middle class in the 1950s and 1960s meant that I, despite my family's background, could aspire to go to Harvard—a symbol of America's broadening acceptance of Jews into elite spaces and places of repute. Through good grades, an athletic background (I played basketball in high school, though not very well; our motto at Madison was "We may be small, but we're also slow"), and 800s on my SATs, I was lucky enough to get in. In the early twentieth century, the number of Jewish students had risen dramatically at Harvard, so much so that a fifth of the Class of 1921–22 was Jewish. But that led to a backlash at Harvard and other elite universities, and for a few years, changes were made to the admission criteria to limit their numbers.

Rarely did I experience antisemitism on Harvard's campus from my friends and peers. Still, there were moments that reminded me that prejudice against Jews had not completely disappeared. As a student, I was dating a young woman named Rosie who worked as a secretary in the admissions office. Perhaps to show off, she said she could get me a copy of my admissions file. I met her one day after class, and a manila folder was on the corner of her desk with my name on it. Written next to my test scores was a note from an admissions officer. I read over her shoulder: "You know how I feel about these New York people"— code for Jews—"but this one may be too smart to reject." To this day, some fifty years later, I remember the name of the man who wrote that note. More significant, I remember the realization I had while reading it: Jews like me could be accepted by the traditional American institutions of power and influence, but there was going to be an element of reservation or reluctance.

THE JEWISH-AMERICAN EXPERIENCE in postwar America was characterized by upward mobility, with more and more entering the middle class and even higher income groups. Compared to the mostly working-class first wave of immigrants, more second- and third-generation American Jews could choose to become not only artists, comedians, writers, and journalists, but also bankers and lawyers and CEOs of big businesses. As the 1950s turned into the 1960s and 1970s and Jews achieved higher economic status, different forms of discrimination, however, took hold. It was not whether Jews would be admitted at all into a profession, but about how many Jews could climb the ladder in that profession. A law firm or hospital, for example, might recruit Jewish lawyers or doctors, but balk at the idea of hiring more than a few (you wouldn't want to be seen as a Jewish firm, after all).

Like many other ethnic groups and women, Jews had to work harder to get and advance in the same jobs as their non-Jewish white colleagues. For decades, Jews were kept out of clubs, associations, and even some white-collar workplaces that signified acceptance and success in American society. A Jewish businessman would not be admitted to his local golf club. Jewish doctors would not be allowed to work at the biggest hospitals. Jewish lawyers were not hired by the prestigious white-shoe law firms. This relatively widespread discrimination led to the founding of several Jewish-led clubs, banks, law firms, hospitals (think of your local "Mount Sinai" or "Beth Israel"), and other businesses by the midtwentieth century. When I was in law school, I worked as a summer associate at Paul, Weiss, one of the rare firms where Jews and Gentiles had worked side by side since its founding. My brother is a partner there today.

Throughout this period, there were some complicated feelings within the Jewish community about these barriers. A handful of Jews made it their goal to be accepted by institutions that deliberately excluded Jews. I knew one man who made it his life's goal to be the first to join the Maidstone Club, a private country club in East Hampton. When he finally did achieve his dream, the reaction from his mostly wealthy Jewish peers was, on the one hand, "It's good that it happened"; on the other hand, it was "What a schmuck." For centuries, Jews have been offered a devil's bargain: trade away your culture and heritage in exchange for acceptance. There's always been a fine line between assimilation and totally losing your identity, and strong opinions about how far Jews should stray on either side of that line. How American should Jews try to become? How American *could* Jews become? These questions were on the minds of the great Jewish-American writers of midcentury America, Saul Bellow and Philip Roth and Bernard Malamud, whose works I read in high school and college.

Things were changing, however, and as the '60s gave way to the '70s and '80s, more of the institutional barriers were being broken down and more Jews were starting to arrive into positions of power. A. M. Rosenthal, for example, became executive editor of the *New York Times*. Henry Kissinger was appointed secretary of state, and Harold Brown secretary of defense. New York City got its first Jewish mayor. The history of Lehman Brothers, in the Stefano Massini play *The Lehman Trilogy*, recounts another such changeover: the titanic struggle between Pete Peterson and Lew Glucksman for control of the firm in 1983. Though the firm was founded by a Jewish family, Pete Peterson, who ran the company in the '70s and early '80s, carried himself like an old-line WASP, despite being a son of Greek immigrants. At the time, finance was a two-tiered system: Investment banking (and its leadership) was a realm populated by preppies, a large proportion of whom were WASPs, whereas the traders on the floor could be from anywhere. I remember a scene that recounted how Pete would walk down the halls of Lehman, writing notes to himself. He would throw them over his shoulder when he was done scrawling, and someone would be following him, ready to collect his discarded shreds of wisdom. Lew Glucksman was his foil, a rough-cut Jewish trader, who scrapped with him for control of the company, eventually taking it over. On Wall Street, it was seen as an epochal shift, a changing of the guard from the old to the new style, with a Jewish trader at the vanguard.

BY THE TIME I was elected to the House of Representatives in 1980, antisemitism was rapidly fading as a force in American society. Being Jewish was no longer a mark or cause for shame or embarrassment within elite institutions, and while most folks still probably regarded Jews as different, it was expressed more as a curiosity about our cultural and religious practices. Sometimes you would hear comments about your Jewishness that sounded off, and maybe carried with them a whiff of suspicion, but almost always it reflected a benign misunderstanding rather than malice or bigotry. For the most part, the worst thing I encountered was confusion.

My first few years in Congress were full of such examples. I was sworn in as a congressman in January 1981, and my extended family piled into a car to make the drive from New York to Washington, DC, including my grandfather, Jack Schumer, one of the Schumers who came to America as a child before the turn of the century, and also Minnie Schumer, my grandmother.

Minnie didn't speak English that well. She had to learn it at the age of twenty when she first came to America in 1914. She *loved* to cook. Her handwritten recipes might as well have been written in stone and delivered from Mount Sinai—they were passed down from generation to generation, and you were not to argue with them. Her chicken was to die for. Minnie married my grandfather, who was her first cousin, which was not unusual in those days but is rightfully no longer recommended for the sake of genetic diversity. Sometimes I wonder if that was the reason I come from such a strange family. They had a long marriage, and she always doted on her three sons, Abe, Harry, and Shelly, or as she called them: Abe-enyu, Har-enyu, and Shell-enyu. "Enyu" is a Yiddish term of endearment, a diminutive, the Old World's way of turning Tom into Tommy or Daniel into Danny.

My grandmother would talk constantly. My grandfather, more of a quiet intellectual type, was less verbose. Minnie would be off on a tangent, talking, talking, talking, and as soon as my grandfather popped his head above the parapet and interjected, she would cut him off. "Jack," she'd snap in her thick European accent, with its Germanic *V*'s, and *H*'s before every word with a vowel at the beginning: "Let me get a verd in hedgevise."

She was chutzpah in flesh and bone, the kind of person who'd strike up a conversation with the person sitting next to her on the bus. When she got to Washington for my swearing-in, that was exactly what she did. Unfortunately for me, it wasn't a humble stranger on public transit. As I waited in line with the other freshmen representatives, I saw my grandmother grab the elbow of the Democratic Speaker of the House, the legendary Tip O'Neill, my new boss, upon whom my political fortunes would depend. Without provocation or invitation, she began to tell him her life's story.

"Ve vere born in a tiny town called Chortkiv in Eastern Europe, but the egg business vent bad," she began. "So ve came to America and ve had no money. I had to valk five miles to get to verk to save a nickel car fare. I got married and raised three boys and they all fought in the War and none of them ran away because they were all breastfed."

She was a big believer in breastfeeding and thought that it was something Tip O'Neill needed to know.

"Isn't America a great country?" she asked him. "My son Abe is an exterminator, he never vent to college, and now his son is being sworn in as a congressman!"

After each little vignette, she punctuated her sentence with an admonition: "Take good care of Chuck-enyu," meaning me, her grandson.

"So the egg business vent bad and ve had to move to America. Take good care of Chuck-enyu."

"I had to valk five miles to get to the sveatshops. Take good care of Chuck-enyu."

"My son Abe is an exterminator, he never vent to college, and today his son is being sworn in as a congressman. Vhat a great country! Take good care of Chuck-enyu."

Eventually, we all got sworn in and I went out to dinner with my whole family to celebrate. The next morning was my first day on the job. I arrived early to an empty office—Congress wasn't so well organized in those days—and I was sitting at my desk, not knowing what to do. There was no schedule.

Only ten minutes had passed when the phone rang. There was no one else to pick it up, so I took the call myself. It was Tip O'Neill's right-hand man, Leo Diehl. He said, "Congressman Schumer, please come over here. Speaker O'Neill wants to see you immediately."

I felt all the fear and confusion of a second grader called

into the principal's office on the first day of school. I racked my brain: "Oh my God, what did I do wrong already?"

When I arrived, the Speaker, a genial, gentlemanly sort, could tell I was nervous. He came over and draped his arm around me.

He said, "Charles, I very much enjoyed meeting your family, particularly your grandmother. What a nice lady! But answer for me one thing: What the hell is a Chuckenyu and how the hell do we take care of it?"

Red-faced but relieved, I explained to him that a Chuckenyu was not some proposed legislation or local issue, but rather the freshman congressman around whom his arm was draped.

I've told that story many times over the course of my life, mostly because it comes with a great punchline. But on reflection, it was a revealing and even profound moment for me. Here I was, a middle-class Jew from Brooklyn, elected to Congress. I was discovering just how much or how little I would be accepted by my new colleagues and especially by the old guard. Would I be dismissed or looked down on or ignored? Would my Jewishness be a problem or a nonissue? I learned that it was neither of those things: My Jewishness was not going to be a major hindrance, but also that it was going to play a role in my political career—my family's history and the legacy of their experience in Eastern Europe were part and parcel of it. My grandmother personified that history and wasted no time imparting it to my boss, the Speaker of the House. I didn't become a member of Congress despite my Jewishness, or because it no longer mattered. It certainly did, and it was always going to be a factor, something my political friends and adversaries would associate with me. But the first major political encounter of my career was a meaningful one. The legendary Speaker of the House, an Irish-American of a very different generation and demeanor but the descendant of immigrants much like my family, recognized something familiar in my grandmother and made it a point to make me feel welcome. Twenty years earlier, I was hearing schoolyard taunts on the streets of Brooklyn. Now I was sitting in the Speaker's office. I was thirty years old.

Throughout my early years in Congress, when my wife and I were invited to social dinners, people tried to be careful about what we could eat and not eat. Do we mind ham sometimes? Or never? What about shellfish? Could we come over on a Friday night? There were plenty of questions, all good-natured, arising from good intentions and a desire to be polite and accommodating, or a simple lack of knowledge, but there was a sense that we were different from most of the other young congressional families. Occasionally, I caught a whiff of the older, nastier attitudes toward Jews. On the day of my first committee meeting, one of the senior Southern congressmen turned to me and said, in his antebellum twang, "Mr. Schumer, welcome to the Jew-diciary Committee."

Still, this was in the midst of a long Golden Age for Jews in America. At Ivy League and elite universities throughout the country, Jews, some of whom had parents who hadn't gone to college, accounted for much greater shares of the student body than we did of the overall population. Sure, Jewish-American parents still celebrated sons and daughters who wanted to become doctors or lawyers, but those preferences and the immigrant practicality that created them had long since gone out of style. Jews could reasonably aspire to any profession and expect that they'd not only be treated fairly but, through hard work and talent, rise to the very top. "The fusion of Jewish culture and American democracy had produced wonders," admired the Israeli Jewish journalist Ari Shavit. "Not only did [America] allow so many Jews to realize their talents and skills—and to arrive at such extraordinary achievements in the sciences, the arts, literature, business, media, academia, film, politics, medicine, and jurisprudence—it allowed the Jewish minority to carve out an enormous, autonomous public space of a size and grandeur that have never been created before, and may never be created again." Jews were now trendsetters and leaders of cultural movements. The author Franklin Foer labeled the '90s the apex of this Golden Age. "The nation's sartorial aesthetic," he wrote in *The Atlantic*, "was the invention of Ralph Lifshitz, an alumnus of the Manhattan Talmudical Academy before he became the denim-clad Ralph Lauren. The national authority on sex was a diminutive bubbe, Dr. Ruth. Schoolkids in Indiana read Anne Frank's diary. The Holocaust memoirist Elie Wiesel appeared on the nightly news as an arbiter of public morality. The most-watched television show was *Seinfeld*. Even Gentiles knew the words to Adam Sandler's 'The Chanukah Song,' which earned a place in the canon of festive music annually played on FM radio." Steven Spielberg's *Schindler's List* won Best Picture at the Oscars in 1994, and in my view, it did more to warn modern generations about the dangers of antisemitism than any other piece of modern media. The Supreme Court had two Jewish justices, and Senator Joe Lieberman was the Democratic nominee for vice president in 2000.

It was during this apogee that I first ran for US Senate, in 1998. The motivation to seek higher office came from many different places. I had found myself to be a natural legislator. I am a social creature at heart. I liked the back-and-forth of negotiations, and I wanted to get things done. In the House, a majoritarian institution, the minority was often trampled over or simply ignored. The Senate's arcane rules and procedures meant that consensus and compromise were almost always required to advance legislation, so you could make a difference no matter how the last election shook out. I thought I'd be good at being a senator, and of course, ambition played a part. But there was something else, too: a feeling that winning a Senate election in a big state like New York would prove something about what Jews could achieve in America. I had always represented a district in Brooklyn, which, though the demographics changed from time to time, was always familiar with or part of the Jewish flavor of New York City (colleagues in the House used to joke that the only other place I could get elected was in South Florida, where many of my Jewish constituents had moved or were planning to move). A statewide race offered a different proposition entirely: rural Republican strongholds in Western New York, vast conservative-leaning areas of Upstate New York; and parts of Long Island that were much more uniformly Catholic and Protestant than the city. I wasn't worried that there was an underlying animus toward Jews in those parts of the state. It's only that as both a politician and a Jew, you have a little voice in the back of your head that wonders, does being a Brooklyn Jew named "Schumer" play as well in places where there aren't many Jews? Adding to the challenge, I was running against a very savvy Republican incumbent, Al D'Amato, who had earned the nickname "Senator Pothole" for his dogged advocacy of local issues over the previous two decades.

Senator D'Amato had a particular strategy for the Democratic candidates he came up against. He would save up his contributions, and as soon as his opponent became official after the primaries, he would race to define him or her with television ads. In the last contest, he'd described his opponent Robert Abrams, also Jewish, as "hopelessly liberal." And his media consultant had created an ad for George Pataki a few years prior with the tagline: "Mario Cuomo, too liberal for too long." Anticipating the deployment of this strategy, one of my closest friends and political advisors, Carol Kellermann, came up with a response. Senator D'Amato had been in office a long time and hadn't always managed to keep his promises. Our response was going to be: "D'Amato: too many lies, for too long." It was tough messaging, but we thought it would give our campaign a chance to hang in there long enough to compete. Less than three weeks before the election, we were running even with Senator D'Amato, and his campaign was feeling the pressure. During a private meeting with Jewish leaders—D'Amato had gotten 40 percent of the Jewish vote in his last two Senate elections, and was afraid of losing many of those votes to me—he called me a "putzhead." "Putz" is Yiddish slang for a certain part of the male anatomy but is maybe best translated as "jerk." It's not terribly insulting in the Jewish vernacular, but it would soon become clear that D'Amato didn't really know the meaning of what he had said.

When reporters confronted him about the pejorative, D'Amato, believing it was much worse of a curse than it actually was, said, "I would never use such a horrible word."

Unsatisfied, the press hounded the New York City mayor,

Ed Koch, a D'Amato supporter who had been in the meeting with him and the Jewish leaders.

Mayor Koch confirmed to the press that he did use that word.

We answered: "D'Amato: too many lies, for too long." The race was over.

It didn't bother me at all that he called me a putz, and I didn't notice any hint of antisemitism in D'Amato. In fact, if he had understood the context and meaning of that word, he might have been able to brush aside the whole controversy. It's hard to know just how much the Jewish element of the insult affected the race, though in my view, it was more about the fact that D'Amato was untruthful versus any sort of disapproving reaction by New Yorkers to his crude language. Still, it was another example of how being Jewish can cause a certain degree of confusion, and a reminder that attitudes toward and about Jews, even when they are mostly positive, never truly lose their salience. Even in the best time for Jews to be Jewish in America, my crowning achievement as a politician was, in some way, impacted by my Jewishness.

FRANKLIN FOER, WHO described the Golden Age for American Jews in an essay in *The Atlantic*, includes a date for when it ended: September 11, 2001. His explanation: the "terror attacks opened an era of perpetual crisis, which became fertile soil where the hatred of Jews took root." As in earlier eras of history when wars and famines, pandemics and economic shocks precipitated social anxiety about the Jews, the last twenty years have produced many of the same disruptions. From the Iraq

War to the 2008 Financial Crisis, the Great Recession, and the Covid pandemic—alongside globalization and the drastic reorganization of the world from analog to digital—the world of the early-twenty-first century looked a lot scarier and more chaotic than the world at the end of the twentieth century. I'm not sure if September 11 was the defining moment that marked the beginning of the end of the best time to be Jewish in America, but when I search my own memory, something began feeling different after those attacks. There was a newfound fear and uncertainty about America's place in the world, which has grown over the past twenty years.

American Jews noticed some of the old conspiracy theories about Jewish power and influence cropping up again. Soon after 9/11, some websites began passing around a theory that it was a plot orchestrated by Mossad, the Israeli intelligence service, or that Jews had advance knowledge of the attack and were told to stay home from work. Nearly 40 percent of non-Jewish-Americans blamed "the Jews" on some level for the financial crisis, according to a survey reported in a 2009 essay in the *Boston Review*. As events in the Middle East were coming into greater focus, anger at Israel began growing at the end of the first decade of the twenty-first century. At universities and among left-leaning groups across the country, the Boycott, Divestment and Sanctions Movement gained visibility and support. While most of the anger was a reaction to Israeli policies in the occupied Palestinian territories and expressed through peaceful protest or speech, in some cases, for the first time it stepped over the line, and Jewish students and Jewish campus organizations like Hillel were targeted. Online conspiracists started to blame Jews for creating "false flag" operations, like the mass shootings at Sandy Hook Elementary School and the Charleston church, so they could take away guns from white Christians. Many American Jews were probably concerned by these trends, and certainly much more aware of them than our non-Jewish friends, but we were not yet on high alert.

And then in 2017 there was a protest in Charlottesville, Virginia, over the proposed removal of a Confederate statue. It featured neo-Nazis and KKK sympathizers marching with tiki torches and chanting white supremacist slogans like "Jews will not replace us." On October 27, 2018, a man walked into the Tree of Life synagogue in Pittsburgh with a semiautomatic rifle to murder Jews. It happened again at a synagogue in Poway, California, in April 2019. A kosher grocery store in Jersey City, New Jersey, was the site of a mass shooting in December 2019. Jews were understandably worried that rising bigotry was beginning to spill over into violence. Still, this was America—the safest country in the world to be Jewish, along with Israel. The overwhelming majority of Jewish-Americans, though concerned that antisemitic violence was now on the rise, nevertheless felt that these were troubling but isolated incidents.

Everything changed on October 7, 2023. When Hamas attacked Israel in the worst instance of mass violence against Jews since the Holocaust, antisemitic incidents in the United States exploded in the weeks and months after. Among other examples, boycotts were organized against many Jewish-owned eateries in Philadelphia. A swastika was graffitied on an iconic Jewish deli on the Upper East Side of my home city. In Thousand Oaks, California, a pro-Palestine protester shouted at Jewish-Americans that "Hitler should've smashed you." Jewish college students who wore a yarmulke or displayed a Jewish star were harassed, vilified, spat on, and attacked on campus. Columbia University was the site of some of the most wrenching scenes and behavior. Last spring, just outside the university gates, a man with his face obscured by a keffiyeh screamed at Jewish students: "Never forget the seventh of October...that will happen not one more time, not five more times, not ten more times, not one hundred more times, not one thousand more times, but ten thousand times!" That's exactly what Jews are afraid of.

There were nearly nine thousand examples of antisemitic incidents in America in 2023, the worst on record since the Anti-Defamation League started keeping count more than forty years prior. A few instances particularly rattled me. In late November of that year, I read about the ordeal of a veteran teacher at Hillcrest High School in Queens, who was forced to hide in a locked office for two hours after hundreds of her fourteen- and fifteen-year-old students ran rampant through the hallways to find her, having learned from her Facebook profile picture that she'd attended a rally supporting Israel in the wake of the terrorist attacks on October 7. I invited her to be my guest when I gave my Senate address on the rise of antisemitism in America the following week, and my heart is still broken for the terror and sorrow she was made to feel.

The events that affected me most, however, occurred in the immediate aftermath of the October 7 terrorist attacks, when Israel had barely begun to mount a military response. However critical someone might have been about Israel as a country or its government policies toward Gaza and the Palestinian territories before October 7, it was deeply disturbing to Jews like me that anyone would treat the loss of Jewish lives so casually, nearly with indifference and even a hint of satisfaction. A handful of civic activists, students, and professors, some at institutions of real repute and standing, referred to the mass slaughter of more than a thousand Israeli Jews as "exhilarating" or "justified resistance," and they labeled the Israel regime itself as "entirely responsible" for the unfolding violence. There were rallies and marches, where hundreds partook, that appeared to be in celebration of what happened on October 7.

As a nation, we can and must have a difficult conversation about where criticism of Israel's military response to the October 7 attacks turns into antisemitism and where it is entirely appropriate. I, myself, have engaged in such criticism, and it's a topic I will cover extensively. But in those very early days after the attack when those rallies and marches took place, there were dead Jews still to be buried, their bodies tortured and mutilated, entire Jewish families and communities slain, the dreadful awareness of Jewish women brutally raped, and Jewish children bound and gagged and dragged into Gaza, some into concrete tunnels to have their lives bargained for or discarded.

To me and to many Jews, the reaction in the immediate aftermath of the October 7 attacks was evidence of a dangerous undercurrent of prejudice and bias that went beyond disputes with Israel's policy. The fact that some in America felt an immediate instinct to ascribe blame not only to Israel but to Jews in America and Jews of all nationalities felt like a warning sign about the state of antisemitism in our country. In the months since, many Jews feel the undercurrent is too quickly becoming a deluge.

JEWS ARE LIVING through the worst period of antisemitism in America in generations. I believe it is connected to the fact that we're living in an age of dislocation and change. There are also identifiable causes, political concepts, narratives, and technologies that have made antisemitism, on the left and the right, far worse than at any point in recent memory. Nativist movements on the political right, for instance, found mainstream expression, first in the vice-presidential candidacy of Sarah Palin and later in the candidacy and presidency of Donald Trump. Movements on the political left, meanwhile, became preoccupied with tearing down structures of power and oppression; often identifying Israel and Jews as part of those structures. At the same time, social media has leapt forward and provided new avenues for very old and unquestionably antisemitic ideas about Jews to be recirculated and reshared and reposted. We'll examine each of these factors in the coming pages, as well as how Israel has become a driving force, and focal point, for generating antisemitism in the twenty-first century.

Could something like a Holocaust happen again in the twenty-first century? It may seem like a crazy question. The Holocaust was so uniquely terrifying. The experience of the Jews in Germany has been so unlike our experience thus far in America and in other countries. But some Jews wonder.

I have a sense that when non-Jews hear Jews warning about the dangers of antisemitism, and how certain ideas and patterns remind us of what happened in Germany in the 1930s, they believe that we are being paranoid or hyperbolic, intentionally overstating the danger Jews face in the world for sympathy or effect. But it's important to understand that Jews have a long memory of the cycle of antisemitism, and it does not only include the horrors of the Holocaust. While it may seem less relevant to compare today's events with the circumstances of ancient Egypt or Rome, or medieval Europe, or nineteenth-century Russia, those places and those time periods are also on our minds, part of our collective memory and inherited trauma. What we've learned from history is that when people are angry and upset, that rage has all too frequently revealed or turned into antisemitism. And so, to many of us, it does not seem ridiculously hyperbolic to question whether the United States, the Promised Land for so many years for so many millions of Jews, might one day succumb to the tidal wave of history—remote as that might be at the present moment. Failing to consider and carefully weigh the possibility doesn't make it any less likely to happen. In fact, it increases the danger.

CHAPTER 5

ANTISEMITISM

Technology, Social Change, and Social Media

Truth be told, I'm online less frequently than you might think. I do check email to read memos, polls, or policy briefings, and I'll use my iPad to watch political ads for Senate Democratic candidates. But I spend far less time on the internet than my friends and peers. Famously to my colleagues and DC reporters, I still use a flip phone. Out of necessity, as I have progressively made the digital transition along with the rest of America, I have experienced, like everyone else, the dark underbelly of the online world. Last year, I was alerted to an account on X (formerly Twitter) called the "Gentile News Network." They had posted a picture of a page from a "physiognomy" and "phrenology" handbook from 1902. These are debunked pseudosciences, the "study" of facial features and skull shape to determine human characteristics like honesty and intelligence. The picture showed profiles of a "deceitful" eye, mouth, chin, and head—all of which looked like classic stereotypes of an Eastern European Jew. Retweeting the graphic, another user had commented: "Never did like Chuck Schumer." I scrolled through the GNN feed on X. Turns out, the post I had seen was relatively tepid.

On many of my social media posts, I'll receive a deluge of antisemitic hate in the replies. My office might post about a new judge who was sworn into office in New York. "Schumer is an elite Jew trying to destroy our country and our values," a typical response would say. "Schumer means 'worthless' in German... look it up," says another (it doesn't). Anytime I express compassion for the victims of a crime in New York, I'll receive such comments as "Jews like you are importing the criminals who are poisoning our country," pictures of Jews in front of Israeli flags and cascading dollar bills, or images of Jews controlling spiders crawling over the globe. Oftentimes, the comments are posted alongside photos of me with my wife and children.

Could my grandson, in years to come, find this kind of antisemitic content, about his own family no less? Absolutely, he could—and worse.

As I tried to understand the rise of modern antisemitism in America, my first instinct was to examine what was happening in our political culture. I'm a politician; politics is my first frame of reference. I wanted to look at what was happening inside political movements on the left and the right that might have caused them to latch on to this ancient prejudice. But before getting to politics, it's important to examine what is happening in our country—economically, socially, morally, and certainly technologically—to get a picture of the underlying conditions that are allowing antisemitism to more easily reemerge. Politics, after all, is often merely a reflection of deeper forces in a society.

This chapter focuses on technology and social upheaval and how they have affected antisemitism through the centuries, most recently through the internet and social media. I want to explore two ways in which technological advancement has contributed to antisemitism, in the world and in America. First, throughout history, technology has increased the speed with which economic, social, and societal change occurs. Technology accelerates changes that would have happened at a slower, more modest pace in society. The increasing pace of change can often cause people to feel like they're losing their grip on a world they once knew. That feeling of confusion, fear, and lack of rootedness is fertile terrain for racism and xenophobia. Especially when world events darken a nation's mood, they can trigger the instinct to cast blame on an "other," often the Jews, for the instability in society. Second, just as technology has created more fear of change in society, which can motivate people to find scapegoats, advances in communications technologies have allowed prejudices and biases to spread more deeply and widely.

Make no mistake, this is not a screed about the perils of technology. In fact, I believe strongly in technology and its enormous benefits to society. Innovation and scientific advancement are overwhelmingly and undeniably positive. Technologies have lifted billions out of poverty and hunger around the globe, and created wealth and levels of comfort and capability our ancestors could scarcely imagine. Americans live longer, healthier, more productive lives, and have more information at our fingertips than any generation living in human history because of technology. But as much as we admire and value technology's benefit, we cannot disregard its negative effects. In our highly advanced information age, we have not yet dealt with the dishonesty, misinformation, hatred, and antisemitism propelled by the internet and social media. Even though the benefits of technology far outweigh the harms, we have an obligation to examine the latter.

THERE ARE MANY historic examples of social change and advances in communications technology that have created conditions that allowed antisemitism to spread, from the Middle Ages to the nineteenth-century French Republic and twentieth-century Europe. These factors don't always converge or occur at the same time, but they often do.

In medieval Europe, antisemitism exploded during a period of great upheaval. The Holy Roman Empire in the 1400s was racked by religious turmoil; there was widespread animosity toward the excesses of the Roman Catholic Church in the lead-up to the Protestant Reformation. The dominant economic model for much of the Middle Ages—feudalism—was straining, and popular discontent was growing. Jews were often a convenient target in this era of social unrest. In addition, the printing press was invented in the midfifteenth century, which allowed for the first time in history the mass production of antisemitic content.

In the 1470s, one such episode played out in the Italian city of Trent, where a young Christian boy named Simon went missing and was later found dead. The city elders held the Jewish community responsible, claiming they used his blood for ritual purposes. Under torture, the Jewish leaders were forced to confess, sentenced to death, and burned at the stake; in addition, all Jewish residents were banished from Trent. What makes this particular story so instructive is that it was seized upon by antisemites with access to a critical new means of spreading their fabrications: Johannes Gutenberg's printing press, a technology that would bring tremendous advancements for humankind but also could be used to negative ends. Whereas old Manetho in Egypt had to rely on a reed pen for writing on papyrus, which was then copied by hand and distributed to a select few, medieval Europe's Jew haters could efficiently replicate their diatribes with a fraction of the time and effort. Information that used to circulate within villages, towns, or cities—which could be reproduced only painstakingly by hand—could now be reproduced en masse and travel far and wide. What was, of course, a novel means of spreading positive messages, like religious doctrine, plays, and songs, also became a channel for transmitting virulent antisemitism. The story of Simon of Trent would be reprinted and illuminated in texts and plays in Central Europe for the next few decades, along with numerous other polemics against the Jews of Europe. The result was predictable. Antisemitism escalated throughout the Holy Roman Empire at the close of the century, leading to a wave of Jewish expulsions of which the Spanish Inquisition is the most famous—but only one—example.

Moving forward, in the late nineteenth century, Emile Durkheim, a French academic considered one of the founding fathers of modern sociology, sought to explain why another period of acute antisemitism had descended upon his country in the wake of the Dreyfus Affair. Alfred Dreyfus was a Jewish French artillery officer who had been falsely accused of selling military secrets to Germany. Forged evidence led to his conviction for treason and a sentence of lifetime imprisonment in 1895. The case would divide French society for years. The Dreyfus Affair was covered breathlessly by the French and international press, which—mindlessly or in bad faith or both—spread the antisemitic lies that ultimately condemned the soldier to his imprisonment. In the mid to late 1800s, commercial journalism was booming, with greater reach and even faster means of production. Highly sensationalized reporting was considered the order of the day, and in the United States as well as France, so-called yellow journalism was ascendent. A *New York Times* article from 1898 described the French press of the time as "vile and venal, and...the models of the yellowest of our own yellow journals. Hardly a word that appears in them is trustworthy." While a campaign to overturn Dreyfus's conviction would eventually succeed in 1906, France, fueled by the antisemitic headlines that gripped a nation, experienced one of the worst periods of antisemitism in its history.

In his 1899 essay "Antisemitism and Social Crisis," Durkheim contended that this latest episode of antisemitism in France was "the consequence and the superficial symptom of a state of social malaise." Durkheim believed that the rapid changes of modern society—industrialization, an overly specialized division of labor, and urbanization—brought about a breakdown of social norms and values, leading to a condition he described as "anomie." In that state, individuals feel detached from social and moral bonds, and they can forget their common links with humanity. People empathize less with others who are not exactly like themselves. Antisemitism becomes a convenient outlet for general anger and frustration. That was why Jews were blamed for the economic crisis that preceded the 1848 revolution, argues Durkheim, as well as France's defeat in the Franco-Prussian War in 1870. Whenever things turned sour in France and pressure started to build, antisemitism became a release valve of sorts, and writers were ever present to distort facts and spread antisemitic stories with increasing commercial and technological efficiency.

As we move into the twentieth century, the same factors keep popping up during periods of severe antisemitism: dramatic social change, national humiliations, economic disasters, and general periods of tumult and technological advancement, inflamed further when a leap forward in the methods of communications and a deterioration in ethical standards occurs at the same time. At a radio exhibition in Berlin in August 1933, the master Nazi propagandist Joseph Goebbels declared that "it would not have been possible for us to take power, or to use it in the ways we have, without the radio." In the 1920s, during the Weimar Republic, the democratic predecessor to the Nazi regime in Germany, radio ownership was limited. Radios were expensive and beyond the means of many German citizens, particularly because the German economy had precipitously tanked in the years after the First World War; the global Great Depression that followed the 1929 Wall Street crash further exacerbated the situation. And so, in the early 1930s, Goebbels approached an electrical engineer to design a cheaper albeit high-quality model, which would be dubbed the People's

Receiver. It went into production in 1933, with all German radio manufacturers being pressured into producing this model. It was also the year Hitler became chancellor. By the end of the year, the People's Receiver accounted for half the sales of all radios in Germany. The following year, it was 75 percent.

After Hitler assumed power, his party took control of the airwaves, enticing listeners with entertainment and using the medium to broadcast his speeches. Nazi propaganda formed the bulk of political programming, as did broadsides against Jewish citizens for their betrayal and role in the humiliation of Germany in the First World War and its aftermath. The Treaty of Versailles required Germany to pay reparations for the damages suffered by Allied nations, which led to a period of hyperinflation. Jews were blamed for both causing and profiteering from the country's economic distress. According to Keith Somerville, author of a book on radio as a propaganda tool, "Hitler made his hatred of the Jews part of everyday discourse on the radio."

While it grew more malicious and strident in the years leading up to the Second World War, antisemitism on the radio can be found from the very early years of the Nazi regime. "Who is the one who does not want the world to be at peace? Who is the one who needs the strife between people to pursue selfish goals?" one regional Nazi leader asked during a broadcast in October 1933. "It is the Jewish people.... It is those people who pretend to be the chosen ones: It was chosen, to be the master in the world! It was chosen, to devour the peoples!" Goebbels had introduced the theme in March of the same year: "Now the times are over...when Jews could empty their dirt and dustbin over German front-line soldiers and over everything that is holy for German people....Now these nation-wrecking forces of Marxism must clear the way for the spirit of national awakening."

Year after year, broadcast after broadcast, Jewish Germans were undermined and villainized. The Nazi regime was unlike others in world history in its total control of the organs of communication in order to propagate antisemitism. The celebrated German focus on efficiency extended even to the promulgation of the world's most ancient hatred. An analysis by social scientists would later find that in the communities where there was greater exposure to Nazi radio propaganda, there was an increase in the number of antisemitic letters sent by citizens to the Nazi newspaper *Der Stürmer*, and also the number of Jews deported to concentration camps because more German citizens in those communities turned Jews in.

Tens of millions of Germans, suffering through dislocating social conditions such as economic depravity, military humiliation, and the loss of national pride, were conditioned through a new technology to tolerate the regime's antisemitism as a matter of daily life. Many swallowed it hook, line, and sinker, and signed up to participate in it. Why did so many Germans willingly participate in such a monstrous atrocity as the Holocaust? Many believe it would have been impossible if not for the Nazis' totalitarian control over communication and information, which brainwashed so many Germans to viciously hate the Jews and wish their extermination.

In the United States in the 1920s and the 1930s, antisemitism was more virulent and unabashed than it ever was before. During that period, there was a backlash to the massive waves of immigration by mostly Eastern European Jews that began in the 1880s and continued into the 1920s; millions had migrated to the United States to escape persecution and find economic opportunity. They lived in tenement buildings in big cities, strived in working-class and factory jobs, and a few eventually became outspoken leaders and organizers in the American labor movement. During the First World War, when the Bolshevik Revolution broke out in Russia, these new immigrants were suspected en masse for harboring radical political tendencies. Overall, isolationist and nativist sentiment grew in America in the years following the war. And then, the Great Depression, which lasted a decade and left millions unemployed, caused a sharp increase in economic and social anxiety, with Jewish bankers and financiers serving as convenient scapegoats. At the same time, just like in Germany, this was the golden age of radio.

In America, the household radio had become a fixture in homes and workplaces by the 1930s. It was a relatively cheap source of entertainment, and also a way to keep up with the news that used to be delivered once a day (if you had a subscription) or purchased at the newsstand. It didn't require as much leisure time as reading the paper. It could be enjoyed passively, while you were working in the garage or preparing dinner. Imagine how different and new that must have seemed, how marvelous. Unlike in Nazi Germany, the radio in the United States was never the province of the state. While regulated, it was a commercial enterprise, a new American West of advertisers and hucksters and entertainers. Prospectors rushed in like the panhandlers of previous generations, and as a result, a wide variety of voices jockeyed for influence. The radio brought popularity to many wonderful reporters, comedians, and musicians. It connected people in ways they had never been connected before and provided a medium for presidents and prime ministers to offer fireside chats, rally their nation, and lift their people's spirits. But into this new medium also came darker figures—manipulative populists and demagogues—who sensed the radio's potential and exploited it.

In America, figures emerged like Charles E. Coughlin, a rabidly antisemitic priest who offered the first Catholic services on the radio. He became known as the "radio priest." At the peak of his popularity in the early 1930s, Father Coughlin's radio shows reached some 30 million Americans, nearly one in four. In response to one of the most vicious attacks on Jews in Germany in the run-up to the Holocaust—what became known as Kristallnacht, the Night of Broken Glass—Father Coughlin blamed the persecution of Jews in Germany on the Jews themselves. Why? According to Father Coughlin, it was because the Jews had persecuted the Christians first. One of the oldest rationalizations for hatred of Jews was refracted through the newest technology of the twentieth century, a flattening of time and space that reflected the overall disruption of society at large. When a radio station refused to broadcast Father Coughlin's next message, his listeners lionized him as a victim of censorship by the "Jewish-controlled media." Fifty years earlier, it would have been impossible to imagine tens of thousands of antisemites gathering at Madison Square Garden. But in the radio age, that kind of mass demonstration became possible—and in February 1939, more than twenty thousand American Nazis rallied together in New York's signature arena.

All too often, in periods of economic, social, and technological disruption—during depressions, wars, and religious uprisings—anxieties in society have led to Jews being identified as the objects of blame. But when that message of blame is accompanied by a new form of communication that allows it to spread farther and faster than ever before, little flares of antisemitism can become brushfires, and sometimes grow into bonfires.

"HISTORY DOESN'T REPEAT itself, but it often rhymes," goes a saying commonly attributed to Mark Twain. In modern, twenty-first-century America, many of the same factors are present that, in the past, led to periods of antisemitism. We live in rapidly changing times, global crises have led to an increase in both conspiracy theories and social unrest, and new forms of communication have emerged that provide hatred and bigotry fresh avenues for expression and amplification. But unlike the past, the pace of technological change over the past few decades is so much faster, and the effects of new forms of communication so much more powerful, I believe the potential for rising antisemitism is unfortunately much greater in twenty-first-century America than twentieth-century America. If the printing press and radio were great strides forward in human communications, social media and the internet are like a quantum leap.

No doubt those technologies have benefited Americans in extraordinary ways, but they have also chipped away at the traditional foundations of society and frayed the social bonds that used to unite us. They've made the changes in the world feel more chaotic, less digestible, and less governable. And they have allowed for bigotry and hatred of all kinds to proliferate online. By increasing social anxieties and frictions and by giving hateful content a new global platform, technology has been affecting modern America—and antisemitism—in ways unlike previous chapters in our history.

Our country has recently become angrier, more divided, less tethered together. It's not in America's nature to be those things. I have always believed that Americans are a big-hearted, forward-looking, optimistic people. Our history is one of risk-taking and entrepreneurialism, constant renewal and reinvention. For most of my political life up to the present, most of my constituents have reinforced my view of the strength of the American character. Whatever the troubles of the day, Americans always express hope for the future, a bedrock belief in better days, brighter times, and generational progress.

But in the last twenty or so years, I have noticed a change in some of my constituents' normally sunny disposition. As social change has accelerated and the social media age entered its third decade, America resembled less and less the America of old. To many Americans, particularly those of an older generation, it feels like the world is spinning faster on its axis. A recent poll by the American Psychiatric Association (APA) found that American adults have become increasingly anxious over the past three years. Among the top reasons for anxiety were "current events," what the APA president described as "living in a world of constant news of global and local turmoil" and the "unprecedented exposure we have to everything that happens in the world around us"; nearly half the people polled had said they were anxious about the "impact of emerging technology on day-to-day life." In 2023, the US surgeon general issued a report that labeled loneliness an "epidemic"—increasing the risk for premature death akin to smoking fifteen cigarettes a day. It cited recent surveys in which about half of American adults reported measurable levels of loneliness. It has reminded me of Emile Durkheim's anomie—the condition in which social norms, values, and expectations have broken down and individuals feel disconnected from each other—which Durkheim believed was an important precursor to antisemitism in society.

These days, when Americans sometimes talk about going back to the good old days or wanting to make America great again, many of them seem to be yearning for a time in America when there was less anomie; a time when we didn't feel like individual atoms bumping into one another but not connected to one another; a time when the old roots of society—family, religion, community—were much stronger.

Among younger people, who have lived with this technology most of their lives and are normally America's most optimistic demographic, I've noticed a growing sense of discomfort and trepidation, too. According to a 2023 study, higher levels of social media use among young Americans relate not only to increases in loneliness, but to "mental distress." The social psychologist and NYU professor Jonathan Haidt in his bestselling book *The Anxious Generation*, examined why we've seen, since 2012, a dramatic increase in rates of anxiety, depression, self-harm, and suicide among teenage boys and girls. Haidt concluded that one of the biggest factors was that they grew up with smartphones instead of flip phones, with high-speed connectivity, front-facing cameras, and social media apps like Instagram and Twitter, where the "like" button created a visible metric for popularity. Today, kids are bombarded by internet content from a very young age, with all its information and also its vile content and vitriol. While it may sound a bit hyperbolic, the 2023 study concluded that "paradoxically 'social' media appears, in effect, to hinder rather than promote people's social wellbeing." Each semester I have lunch with my Senate interns—high school and college students—and I ask them the same question: Do you think social media has more of a positive or negative impact on society? In recent years, surprisingly, among an age group fully conversant in social media, the majority of them have said it was negative.

The internet age has also completely fractured how Americans get their news and information about the world, isolating us further rather than giving us a shared experience. Fifty years ago, in the second half of the twentieth century, we had what was in effect a national town hall meeting every night at six o'clock. By the mid-1960s, 90 percent of American households owned a television set, and 90 percent of those were tuned to either the ABC, CBS, or NBC evening newscasts. At its peak, in 1980, network television reached more than 52 million viewers, almost a quarter of the entire country at the time. You watched CBS if you liked Walter Cronkite, or NBC if you preferred Chet Huntley and David Brinkley, but ideology had nothing much to do with your preference. So the next day at the office watercooler, no matter which channel you watched the night before, everyone talked about current events citing the same essential facts.

Today, there's a world of difference. The viewer of Fox News is on a different factual planet than the MSNBC viewer. Advances in technology have caused fragmentation in media, with a proliferation in stations and channels, each with their different viewpoints and different facts, each catering to their select, narrow audience, creating echo chambers that exacerbate the partisan divide that now characterizes America.

The same fragmentation occurred with major newspapers.

Technology has allowed millions to easily access online news sources with their distinct partisan slants and often with their own set of facts. According to Pew Research, 86 percent of Americans get their news from smartphones, tablets, or computers at least some of the time; 58 percent of Americans prefer to get their news from websites or apps; 32 percent prefer TV; 6 percent prefer radio. And only 4 percent prefer print. Everyone has found themselves in their own corner, without a common ground of agreed-upon facts. Arthur Miller once quipped, "A good newspaper, I suppose, is a nation talking to itself." Our nation is no longer talking to itself. We're not even speaking the same language.

ALL OF THIS fragmentation has created more fertile ground for antisemitism in America. It has made Americans more anxious, angry, and lonely, and at the same time, social media has given antisemites a bigger platform to exploit the anxiety in our country and turn it toward antisemitism. There are several ways the unique structure of social media allows antisemitism to spread. First, its enormous scale. Second, its lack of editorial control. Third, its power to aggregate individuals who might have some bigoted thoughts but in prior eras would feel alone in or ashamed to publicly express their views, but in their aggregation feel emboldened. And fourth, the ability to post anonymously on its platforms.

Scale

THERE ARE MORE than 5 billion social media users worldwide, nearly two-thirds of the world's population. TikTok alone has more than a billion active users; half of the American population is on TikTok. Half of all Americans also use Instagram. More than two-thirds use Facebook. Eight in ten use YouTube. Antisemitic content, which used to exist in dark corners of American society, can now reach unfathomably large audiences instantaneously in the form of videos, posts, images, or comments. In 2020, a TikTok video with an antisemitic song joking about the Jews killed in Auschwitz, was viewed 6 million times before the post was taken down. Moreover, according to social media experts interviewed by the *Washington Post*, "hateful rhetoric that appears on X ripples out to the whole internet, normalizing an unprecedented level of antisemitic hate."

Holocaust denialism has been around for a while as a tool for extreme antisemites to delegitimize Jewish suffering and smear the Jewish people as liars and fraudsters, but like most antisemitic conspiracy theories, it has mostly existed on the radical fringes of our society. But no longer, thanks in large part to the new levels of exposure the internet provides it. Roughly half of millennial and Gen Z respondents to a nationwide survey in 2020, aged eighteen to thirty-nine, said they had seen Holocaust denial or distortion posts online, and even more reported seeing Nazi symbols on social media or in their communities in the last five years. According to a 2023 online poll by YouGov and *The Economist*, 20 percent of young Americans aged eighteen to twenty-nine believe the Holocaust is a myth. Another 30 percent were not *sure* if the Holocaust was a myth. That means half of all young Americans reached by the poll had substantial doubt about whether the Holocaust, the largest and most-studied genocide of the twentieth century, was a real event. One cannot begin to understand Jewish feelings about

Israel and antisemitism if one denies or is ignorant about the Holocaust.

Lack of Effective Content Moderation

UNLIKE PRIOR COMMUNICATION technologies, social media was designed as a carrier for user-generated content with essentially no editors. When most Americans got their information from traditional news sources, they could be reasonably sure it was more or less based on facts. Editors oversaw the news reporting, and editorial standards, journalistic ethics, and rules for sourcing—such as having two, nonanonymous sources before news could be printed—were guardrails that kept information that was totally bigoted, false, or inflammatory from entering the national conversation. A bigoted or antisemitic comment by a public official or fringe actor was generally not broadcast on TV or radio or reprinted in the newspaper, and if it was, it was surrounded by proper context. Editors of the old-style media, for instance, would have never given a lying bigot like Alex Jones a platform.

On the internet and social media, however, nearly anything goes, and it has led to a documented rise in Americans' exposure to misinformation, disinformation, and conspiracy theories—a few of the canaries in the coal mine of antisemitism. That aspect of social media is part of its innate structure. It was designed as a platform, not a news provider. And its credo is to let anyone post whatever they want. In such a medium, editors don't exist in many places, and where they do, they face an uphill battle. It's not a coincidence that online is where anti-Jewish conspiracy theories originated after 9/11. Online is where you'd find forums that blamed the 2008 financial crisis on an international Jewish banking conspiracy. Online is where conspiracy theories about Jews as creators, spreaders, and beneficiaries of the Covid-19 pandemic circulated freely.

There was a period, especially after Donald Trump's defeat in the 2020 election, during which social media companies decided to regulate content more forcefully on their sites, and some developed stronger terms of service and tools to flag posts that are controversial or contain misinformation. They made clear, for instance, that Donald Trump's claim that the 2020 election was stolen was a lie. But the American right waged a largely successful campaign to push back against those rules in the name of "free speech"—I would call it lying—and most of the companies backed off, with some devastating consequences. Elon Musk's takeover of Twitter provides a case study. He proudly proclaimed that Twitter under his leadership would not regulate content (and would be named X). Since Elon Musk loosened the content moderation guidelines regarding hate speech and disinformation, expressions of bigotry have soared on the platform. In the month following the October 7 attacks in Israel, antisemitic content on X increased by more than 900 percent, according to the Anti-Defamation League.

Despite the pushback from the hard right, most of the major social media companies are aware of the ongoing problem of hate speech online, and to their credit, many try to limit obviously bigoted content. Unfortunately, these efforts have proven all too difficult to enforce. The sheer scale of these platforms and billions of posts makes moderating content a very difficult task to begin with. Determining what specific content violates the terms of service is also an ever-evolving challenge. Making it even harder is the fact that racists and bigots are extremely creative in their expressions of racism and bigotry. In just the last fifteen years, online antisemites have developed numerous strategies for hiding their message in coded language, symbols, or obscure pictures. In the early 2010s, neo-Nazi groups online would tell followers to "read *Siege*," an obscure reference to a violently antisemitic text published in the 1980s that described a "healthy state" as one that will "expel—or kill—the Jew." Another trend was for antisemites to identify something or someone online as Jewish by enclosing it within three parentheses, referred to as an "echo"—(((Chuck Schumer))), for example. Its use started surging in spring 2016, though anti-hate activists, Jewish or not, began to subvert its message by voluntarily putting "echoes" around their own names. Most recently, social media sites have struggled to identify and react to the antisemitism that has exploded online in the wake of the October 7 attacks. Who, for example, a few years ago could have anticipated that the image of a paraglider—an image meant to celebrate the Hamas attackers who paraglided over the Israeli border to murder innocent Jews—would be used to express antisemitism worldwide?

Aggregation

ONE OF THE greatest powers of social media is its capacity to bring people together around ideas, scientific endeavors, activities, and common likes and desires. A page that brings together scientists studying pancreatic cancer or Yankee fans is undeniably a good thing. I still remember an encounter I had in the very early days of social media. I spend most of my weekends away from Washington at home in Brooklyn, where my favorite weekend activity is to take a few hours for a meandering bike ride. About twenty years ago, I was riding past the soccer fields where my little daughters used to play for their AYSO soccer team every Saturday morning. I saw about twenty-five people—a total mixture, old and young, male and female—playing a match. I thought, *What kind of a team is this?* As my grandmother Minnie probably would have done, I pulled my bike up alongside the field and I asked one of the guys warming up, "What league are you playing for?"

He said, "This isn't a league, this is a Meetup."

In the early 2000s, Meetup was brand new. I had never heard of it before, and the soccer player could tell. He told me it was an app—one of the first—that helped connect people online who wanted to come together and discuss a book, converse about an interest, or play a game. I was deeply enamored with the idea that the internet could bring together dozens of people, each of whom might otherwise be sitting at home on the couch, spread across Brooklyn, all having the same desire—to play soccer that afternoon. Previously, they had no easy means of making it happen. I thought, *Wow, this social media thing is going to be fantastic.*

For millions of people, it was and is. Social media has brought together long-lost family and friends, helped businesses reach their consumers in new ways, and public servants reach their constituents. It has spurred astonishing scientific collaborations and expanded professional networks. The benefits to society are manifold and continue to evolve. Twenty-two years after it was founded, Meetup has more than sixty million users worldwide.

But the same connective power of social media allows peo-ple who want to share negative opinions and activities to find each other, too. In the pre-internet age, groups that regularly trafficked in antisemitism or other prejudices were diffuse, decentralized, and rarely coordinated. Social media has made it much easier for them to connect and give one another encour-agement and direction. Before, if an antisemite was sitting at home, alone on the couch, they had very few places they could go to find a fellow traveler. Now, with a flick of the thumb or a click of the mouse, they can go online and meet up. In the years since Meetup was introduced, forums, blogs, and chat groups have cropped up in the darker corners of the internet. 4Chan, Gab, Parler, Bitchute, and Odysee all regurgitate antisemitic content. For example, "The Happy Merchant"—a vile cartoon of a scheming Jewish moneylender—has been one of the most popular memes on 4Chan and Gab. Today, regular contribu-tors to 4Chan and other alt-right/white supremacist platforms actively collaborate to spread antisemitism online. In the weeks after October 7, for example, they started a campaign to post as many "AI Jew memes" as possible on mainstream sites like X, such as images of US soldiers kneeling before a Jewish man on a throne, or Taylor Swift in a Nazi uniform sliding a Jewish man into an oven. The aggregative power of social media allows people who might otherwise be too afraid or too embarrassed to share a controversial or hateful opinion to find others who would. When you see someone else online saying what you're thinking—even if they are a troll or a bot—you feel vindicated and may become convinced that you are not alone, embolden-ing you to post those views online.

Anonymity

ANOTHER DRIVING FORCE of antisemitism online is the ability to share opinions without responsibility or attribution. Things you wouldn't dare say out loud, let alone on television or in print, you can now post anonymously without personal repercussions. Studies have shown that anonymity makes online groups of like-minded individuals more extreme in their discussions and reduces the social pressure that normally holds people back from publicly expressing intolerant, racist, or bigoted ideas. In the wake of the October 7 attacks, anonymous messaging apps on college campuses like Yik Yak and Sidechat featured alarming amounts of anti-Jewish and anti-Israel sentiments, including death threats against Jewish students. In my opinion, anonymity is one of the main reasons why social media platforms, message boards, and comment sections are so full of racist, violent, and antisemitic content, and why Americans are exposed to so much more of it.

As a result of these characteristics, according to a study by the Online Hate Prevention Institute and Online Hate Taskforce, antisemitic content online has increased fivefold since October 7.

I BELIEVE IN Sigmund Freud's concepts of the id, ego, and superego. Every human has emotional impulses and desires, what Freud called the id. Freud believed these impulses were often sexual in nature but could also fall into various categories, not all of them bad, but which include the impulse toward racism, hatred, and xenophobia, and a darker instinct to vilify others for your problems. Freud also believed in a superego, or conscience: moral codes of conduct we obtain from our society and internalize. The superego holds in check our worst, ignoble, and societally destructive impulses. Without a strong superego and a rational ego, our id can run amok, encouraged sometimes by both bigots and opportunists.

Unfortunately, the dizzying pace of societal and technological change over the past few decades seems to have weakened our collective superego, at least when it comes to communications. The newspaper editor who would strike out falsehoods and censor bigoted comments might have been laid off or is too busy supervising the multiple streams of content that journalistic outlets are now expected to churn out. The neighbor who would have admonished an individual for voicing an unsavory opinion is gone, because the purveyor of the opinion is now anonymous. The isolated individual with racist feelings—who would keep those thoughts to themselves because no one would ratify them—is no longer isolated.

There is no doubt that technology, social change, and social media have increased the amount of antisemitism in our society. What troubles me and many Americans is that there are no easy solutions. Communications platforms are larger, more diffuse, and harder to regulate and moderate than at any time in human history. The propensity of social media to circulate incendiary content and even hate speech appears to be written into the very code. And like prior advances in information technology, it would be both impossible and misguided to try to stuff the genie back into the bottle. What must be undertaken instead is an effort to understand how American society can best manage the risks of this new era of information and how it pertains to antisemitism.

I take comfort in the lessons of history. In prior eras, societies eventually adjusted to the advent of the printing press, mass journalism, the radio, and television. Over time, people get better at identifying the weaknesses of their news environment and become less susceptible to propaganda, falsehoods, and deliberate misinformation. Individuals become savvier users and consumers of communication technologies, usually propelled by a national conversation about the risks as well as the rewards of those forms of communication. Sometimes that process can take years, even many decades. But I believe that by grappling with these issues—and sounding a warning—we can speed the process along, and steel more Americans to face the challenge that online antisemitism poses to our country.

CHAPTER 6

ANTISEMITISM ON THE RIGHT

Near center court at Madison Square Garden, where today the electric orange-and-blue New York Knicks logo adorns the parquet, there once stood a three-story-tall banner of George Washington flanked by swastikas. On February 20, 1939, the German American Bund, a pro-Nazi organization in the United States founded a few years prior, held a massive rally in the heart of New York City. Billing the event as a "Mass Demonstration for True Americanism," the Bund drew in twenty-two thousand members carrying signs that read "Wake Up America. Smash Jewish Communism" and "Stop Jewish Domination of Christian Americans."

The event opened with "The Star-Spangled Banner" and a declaration by the first speaker that "if George Washington were alive today, he would be friends with Adolf Hitler." The speakers of the night decried the evils of Jewish influence on

Hollywood and the media. The keynote speaker, Fritz Kuhn, the Bundersführer, denounced President "Frank D. Rosenfeld" and NYC District Attorney Thomas "Jewey," and told the assembled crowd that "you all have heard of me through the Jewish-controlled press. Wake up, you Aryan, Nordic, and Christians, to demand that our government be returned to the people who founded it!" He exited the stage to the thrum of twenty-two thousand American Nazis chanting "Free America, Free America, Free America," their arms raised in stiff salute. It was the largest Nazi rally in American history, at the epicenter of the most Jewish city in the United States. It occurred only eighty-five years ago, during a time when a world war was on the horizon and the country had yet to emerge from a long period of economic downturn and instability.

That night, some Jews fought back, including one twenty-six-year-old plumber named Isadore Greenbaum who'd made it inside and ran onstage to interrupt Kuhn's keynote speech. Greenbaum was beaten senseless by the Bund's uniformed stormtroopers. Jews were also among the hundred thousand counterprotesters gathered outside the arena. Still, those twenty-two thousand American fascists are a part of our history. When I learned about the event—in early adulthood, since it was not a part of mainstream high school education—I was shocked at the number of Nazi supporters who had gathered at the Garden. I think most Americans have never heard about that event, in part for good reason. By the year's end, Kuhn was arrested and sent to prison for embezzlement, and the Bund dissipated in the years after. Though sympathy for fascist ideologies and antisemitism had been on public display in America during the 1930s, and a few famous men like

Henry Ford, Joseph Kennedy, and Charles Lindbergh had been propagating lies and conspiracies on its behalf, America entering the war post–Pearl Harbor brought it all to an end. While there are only limited parallels between 1939 and today, when I look back on that relatively short chapter in American history, I am struck by how many of the comments made at the rally in 1939 have been repeated by right-wing extremists in recent years.

Antisemitism has always found a natural home on the hard right. Ultranationalism, isolationism, an aversion to immigration, and an enthusiasm for racial purity—animating forces of rightward movements in the early twentieth century—run parallel to many age-old, sometimes contradictory, prejudices about Jews as traitors, internationalists, "greedy capitalists," refugees, and agents of disease or "racial pollution." While American Nazis represented the epitome of right-wing antisemitism, they certainly didn't invent it. The bigotry that inspired Adolf Hitler, his party, and its American counterpart was already in the intellectual bloodstream of the West, and it has outlived the Third Reich. Although it was never proven, a bar in a very conservative neighborhood in Queens was rumored to celebrate Hitler's birthday every year, on into the twenty-first century.

Today, we hear language reminiscent of Nazi propaganda, not because far-right extremists want to go back in time to Hitler's Germany (though some might), but because they believe many of the same ideas that Hitler believed: That Jews are evil and seditious, a threat to the racial makeup of their nation, conspirators who seek to corrupt governments and orchestrate world affairs. Those ideas are the ones we must examine in order to understand how and why antisemitism thrives on the political right well into the twenty-first century.

To MANY JEWISH-AMERICANS, antisemitism on the right seems to take two very different forms, expressed by two very different types of antisemites. One aspect of right-leaning antisemitism was the kind expressed by certain rich and powerful WASPs who believed Jews were a threat to a social order that in their minds had naturally and rightly placed WASPs at the top. This was the antisemitism of the private golf club, the suburban dinner party, the white-shoe law firm, and the State Department of the '30s and '40s. It was the dismay over a son or a daughter bringing home a Jewish beau. This was genteel antisemitism. It was exclusionary and discriminatory, yes, but it was almost never violent. To some old-line WASPs, Jews were a fly in the ointment, a misplaced screw in the cogs of the social machinery they had built to elevate their sons and daughters into America's positions of privilege. Their response was not to advocate for our expulsion or extermination; it was to raise barriers at the office and the university, to make snide comments and crass jokes, and to ensure you would never have to bump into a son of Abraham on the eighteenth green.

The other style of antisemitism on the right, however, has been much more virulent, vicious, and familiar to Jews around the world. It is the antisemitism of the populist far-right parties and the alt-right, the neo-Nazis and Ku Klux Klan members and white nationalists who believe that Jews are a threat, not to elite social hierarchies but to racial hierarchies, to society and the nation itself. This kind of antisemitism wallows in conspiracy theories and traffics in racism and hatred, against Black people and immigrants and Muslims and the LGBTQ community as well as Jews. This is the antisemitism of Charlottesville and Pittsburgh and Poway. You might say the difference between the two strains of right-leaning antisemitism is the difference between the white collar and the brown shirt.

It goes without saying, but Jews, and societies in general, have far more to fear from the violent, sometimes lethal antisemitism of the extreme right than the more genteel version. While white-collar antisemitism has largely fallen out of fashion as American society became more accustomed to seeing Jews as CEOs, deans, and heads of organizations, the antisemitism of the far-right continues to attract a small, hardened, and growing core of support. They are perhaps limited in numbers now, but history has shown that their ideology can easily metastasize. Their ideas are seen in several different corners of modern society, and they have a few defining features.

The belief in an ethnic nationalism is one such feature, and it is probably the most dangerous. The Nazi Party articulated this belief with the German phrase "Blut und Boden," a rallying cry that dates back to the 1920s, linking the idea of the "racial purity" of the supposedly superior "Aryan" race with the prosperity of the Fatherland. Those same words, "Blood and soil," were chanted in English by white supremacists at the Charlottesville rally in 2017. Jews had long been viewed in many European societies as a threat to the nation, as outsiders or interlopers who don't truly belong. Arguably, the prejudice's origins lie in the idea of the "wandering Jew," a trope based on early Christian mythology that Jews are destined to wander the Earth as punishment for taunting Christ on his way to the crucifixion. In nineteenth-century Europe, when nationalism was on the rise, and nation-states were being established, the fact that Jews lacked a homeland of their own further reinforced this idea of Jewish "rootlessness." Ruth Wodak, an academic who has written about the radical right and antisemitism, says that "the effect of this prejudice is to suspect Jews of not being wholly reliable with regard to their loyalty to the nation-state.... Jews were regularly regarded as aliens within nations, and sometimes as 'parasites.'" When, today, you hear antisemites referring to Jews as "globalists" or "internationalists," it undoubtedly has its roots in this historical narrative.

To the hard-right ethnonationalist, Jews also present a threat to a nation's racial stock. In Europe, slander about Jews as carriers of disease and infestation and plague are thousands of years old. (Ironically, because Ashkenazi Jews were confined to ghettos for so long and expected to marry only within their own community, Jews now have a higher risk for several genetic disorders, from Tay-Sachs to Crohn's disease.) Nineteenth- and twentieth-century intellectual movements, from social Darwinism to eugenics, elevated negative conceptions of the Jews as an "inferior race." The eugenics movement in the United States was a particularly sordid chapter. At one point it led to forced sterilizations, and twenty-seven states passed laws designed to curtail the number of "genetically unfit" populations, including African-Americans, Jews, and the mentally ill. In the 1920s a prominent eugenicist, Harry Laughlin, served as an expert advisor to the House Committee on Immigration and Naturalization. Across the Atlantic, a young Adolf Hitler looked on admiringly. In *Mein Kampf*, published in 1925 during the Weimar Republic, he wrote: "There is today one state in which at least weak beginnings toward a better conception [of immigration] are noticeable. Of course, it is not our model German Republic, but [the United States]." In the following decade, the Nazis would adopt many of the eugenics policies first practiced in the United States.

Ultimately, the strongest feature of antisemitism on the right is a conspiratorial understanding of the world. A 2023 study conducted on antisemitism in the UK found that British residents most likely to hold antisemitic views are those with a preference for authoritarian governments, people who want to overthrow the established social order, and especially those who believe in "malevolent global conspiracies." Unlike antisemitism on the left, which may from time to time brush against it, antisemitism on the right is steeped in conspiratorial thinking and latches on to obscure texts, from the *Protocols of the Elders of Zion* to its contemporary corollary, *The Great Replacement*, a French text that gave rise to a theory about a Jewish plot to weaken Western societies by literally replacing their white citizens with Black and Brown immigrants. Narratives about Jews pulling the strings of global banking and controlling the media, Hollywood, the Federal Reserve, Western governments, and even the weather are all more prominent on the right.

Many of the beliefs held by the extreme right are so extreme that it can make them easy to dismiss with a scoff. Surely, we think, these outrageous theories can't be terribly widespread. A few decades ago, we could have considered ourselves safe in that assumption. But the internet has made conspiracy theories easier to disseminate and thus harder to ignore. Disinformation and misinformation and the ease with which documents and video can be falsified have made them harder to puncture. Nationalism as a political force has been exceedingly powerful in history, in both democratic and autocratic societies, and its reemergence in the tech-dominated twenty-first century in a belligerent, nativist, and populist form has breathed life into age-old antisemitic tropes. QAnon, the extremely odd internet-era conspiracy theory, alleges that a cabal of prominent Democrats and Hollywood celebrities are running a child sex-trafficking ring at the behest of "global elites" (code for Jews such as George Soros and the Rothschilds) who want to harvest the blood of these children. The QAnon crazies may be using extremely modern technologies to spread their wild fabrications, but the idea that Jews are a threat to children dates back to the blood libel, a medieval canard that Jews use the blood of children in our religious rituals. Video-sharing websites like BitChute and Odysee that publish racist, antisemitic, and conspiratorial content have racked up millions of views, as have videos with QAnon hashtags on TikTok. QAnon quickly transcended the internet to become a cultish far-right movement. In 2021, QAnon devotees were among the insurrectionists who attacked the Capitol on January 6.

A recent survey of the general public by YouGov tested which conspiracy theories Americans believe to be likely true, from the one about the moon landing being staged to the one about Lee Harvey Oswald, JFK's assassin, not being a lone actor. Nine of the ten conspiracy theories presented in the poll were considered by at least 20 percent of the respondents to be definitely or probably true. Forty-one percent also believed in "a broader theory: that regardless of who is officially in charge of the government and other organizations, there is a single group of people who secretly control events and rule the world together." We can no longer dismiss far-right antisemitism just because it has tended to exist on the poles.

WHEN IT COMES to right-wing antisemitism, what Jews fear most is the prospect of it being co-opted by leaders for political gain, giving it the veneer of acceptability and allowing it to move from extreme corners of society into the mainstream. We have to be alert when prominent figures or politicians use antisemitic language or themes, lest it become normalized.

Until recently, those moments had been few and far between, and mostly behind closed doors. President Richard Nixon, for example, was caught on audio tapes complaining to his chief of staff, in almost pantomime Nixonian fashion, that "the Jews are all over the government…you can't trust the bastards; they turn on you." The ultraconservative Republican Pat Buchanan, the White House communications director under Reagan and a nationally syndicated columnist and TV commentator, pondered the complexity of a man like Hitler, complained about "all this wallowing" over the Holocaust, and described Capitol Hill as "Israeli-occupied territory." Buchanan himself ran in the Republican presidential primaries in 1992—against the incumbent George H. W. Bush—and again in 1996, receiving 21 percent of the vote but losing out to Bob Dole. A few hard-right Christian conservatives would also occasionally make news for antisemitic comments. In 1999, Rev. Jerry Falwell, the televangelist and founder of the Moral Majority, said that the anti-Christ was probably "alive somewhere today" and "of course, he'll be Jewish."

A good number of American Jews were aware of those comments and those figures. During an era in which antisemitism was slowly but surely being relegated to the margins, however, we felt that a few right-wing politicians and pastors couldn't do much harm. They might have been reminders that antisemitism was still around, but we took comfort in the fact that it was certainly not acceptable in mainstream America, or even in mainstream conservative politics to openly espouse antisemitic views. But then, starting around the end of George W. Bush's second term, I started seeing a name pop up in right-wing media that had previously received little attention: George Soros.

Mr. Soros had been a hugely successful investor throughout much of the '70s, '80s, and '90s. He had some detractors—and some defenders—in the financial industry, and occasionally was the target of media attention for some of his big financial positions, as well as for his philanthropic work that supports democracy and human rights activism around the world. But around 2008, the hard right in America began invoking his name as the author of the problems plaguing our country. It is not a coincidence that this started to occur right around the time of the financial crisis and the Great Recession.

The year 2008 was an inflection point for antisemitism in the twenty-first century. As if by instinct, during a period of economic disaster, a few folks on the American right reached for a Jewish figure in finance to blame, drawing on age-old stereotypes. The difference this time was that it wouldn't remain only a few. Franklin Foer recounts the American right's obsession with the Soros myth in *The Atlantic*: "After 2008...the right settled on a Jewish billionaire as their villain of choice: George Soros. An idea took hold, and not just on extremist blogs. The right-wing Republican Party seeded the image of Soros as the 'shadow puppet master,' in the words of the former Fox News host Bill O'Reilly. In elevating the figure of Soros and invoking him so frequently, Fox News and Republican politicians were also, intentionally or not, drawing on the deeply implanted imagery of the Jewish financier bankrolling the destruction of Christian civilization."

Today, there is an entire Wikipedia page dedicated to George Soros conspiracy theories: that he was a Nazi collaborator who stole the property of other Jews; that he precipitated a financial crisis in southeast Asia; that he was behind the migrant crisis in Europe and was involved in a secret plot to overturn the Brexit referendum. Hard-right activists and bloggers accuse him of bankrolling immigrant caravans from Central America and paying "crisis actors" to pretend to be students who survived the mass shooting at Marjory Stoneman Douglas High School in Parkland, Florida.

The emergence of Soros as a magnet for right-leaning conspiracists has revealed something about the state of American antisemitism in the 2000s. In the 1960s or 1970s, I believe no prominent media personality or politician would have dared make a Jewish billionaire the object of ridicule or the linchpin of a political argument. They would have been uncomfortable with being labeled antisemitic, and the memory of the Holocaust was still too fresh. But by 2008, Jews were much more secure. It became tolerable, if not acceptable, to cast blame on a single Jewish billionaire even if it might, in the minds of some, increase antisemitic feelings.

A few years later came the now-infamous "great replacement" theory. In 2011, a reactionary French writer named Renaud Camus, no relation to the famous poet, published *The Great Replacement,* in which he argued that a left-wing globalist elite is conspiring to replace Europe's white majority with Black and Brown Muslim immigrants who reproduce faster than the native whites. The great replacement theory essentially took the antisemitic conspiracy theories that have been floating around since the late 1800s and merely updated them for the twenty-first century. Like in ages past, a few of the early American converts to the theory were zealots. Just like Henry Ford funded the publication and distribution of the *Protocols of the Elders of Zion,* Steve King, a Republican congressman from Iowa, repurposed ideas and language from the great replacement theory. In 2017, he tweeted a quote by the far-right Hungarian prime minister, Viktor Orbán: "Mixing cultures will not lead to a higher quality of life but a lower one." In another tweet, King wrote, "We can't restore our civilization with somebody else's babies." Most of my Republican colleagues were horrified by King's tweets, but he was stripped of his committee assignments only in 2019 after he wondered out loud, during an interview, why the terms "white supremacist" and "white nationalist" had become "offensive."

After King lost the primary in his reelection bid in 2020, others picked up the mantle. In 2022, Republican Senate candidates in Arizona and Missouri, Blake Masters and Eric Schmitt, both accused Democrats of "trying to change [the demographics] of our country" by flooding the nation with millions of illegal immigrants; Schmitt won his race. JD Vance, a Senate candidate at the time and now vice president, said that

Democrats "have decided that they can't win reelection in 2022 unless they bring a large number of new voters to replace the voters that are already here." Wisconsin senator Ron Johnson called replacement theory "the Democrat grand plan." Recently, I've noticed that fewer and fewer numbers of my moderate Republican colleagues criticize these kinds of comments. The members of Congress who traffic in these tropes are certainly not antisemites, but they are propagating dangerous theories that in the past have bred antisemitism.

The election of Donald Trump to the presidency in 2016 gave many American Jews another reason to worry. There were a few egregious examples of the Trump campaign coming close to the line of antisemitism, most notably in its closing election ad in 2016, which featured the images of George Soros, then–Federal Reserve chair Janet Yellen, and then–Goldman Sachs CEO Lloyd Blankfein while audio of Trump blamed "global special interests" in cahoots with the "political establishment" for bleeding the country dry. Those three have been important figures in international finance, yes, but otherwise the main thing they have in common is that they are all Jews. Still, the reason a good number of Jews feared a rise in antisemitism under Trump was because he tolerated and sometimes praised leaders of the far-right. Let me state unequivocally: I do not believe Donald Trump is an antisemite. But he all too frequently has created the feeling of safe harbor for far-right elements who unabashedly or in coded language express antisemitic sentiments.

In the run-up to the 2016 election, Donald Trump was asked if he would disavow white supremacists like David Duke—a former grand wizard of the KKK and well-known antisemite—who had professed support for his campaign.

Trump's initial response was to pretend to "know nothing about white supremacists." The "Unite the Right" rally in Charlottesville, Virginia, took place during the first year of his presidency. Neo-Nazis marched through the university campus of a major American city chanting "Jews will not replace us"—a direct reference to the poisonous language that is the great replacement theory—and clashed with counterprotesters, killing a young woman by mowing her down with a car. The president famously said there were "very fine people, on both sides" about an incident in which one of the sides included neo-Nazis. In 2017, the now-infamous white supremacist Nick Fuentes started his livestream show called "America First with Nicholas J. Fuentes," which gained a cult following. Among several antisemitic rants, Fuentes engaged in Holocaust denial and complained that he was witnessing a "bastardized Jewish subversion of the American creed." Trump would later meet Fuentes at a dinner with Kanye West, another noted antisemite, in 2022. When Trump was confronted about Fuentes's presence, he said that he didn't know Kanye was planning to bring him. He never denounced Fuentes or his views, and still hasn't. A year after the dinner, Fuentes called for the mass execution of "perfidious Jews" and other non-Christians.

In my view, just like human beings have an id, an ego, and a superego, so, too, does society. There is always an unfortunate amount of racism, bigotry, tribalism, and hatred of the Other in any society, even in multiracial, multicultural, and multireligious ones. Like individuals, social and political systems need superegos as well to suppress the expression of baser instincts. In modern times, American presidents, much to their credit, have acted like the Freudian superego to the darker id of American politics, a conscience that tries to hold it in check. In the past, whenever American presidents—Democrat and Republican, liberal and conservative—saw outright bigotry, they tried to counteract it or speak out against it. This would certainly apply to most of our recent presidents: Presidents Barack Obama, George W. Bush, Bill Clinton, George H. W. Bush, Ronald Reagan. Unfortunately, we cannot say the same about Donald Trump.

FOR OUR ENTIRE lives, American Jews of my generation have known that if someone was going to walk into our homes or synagogues with a gun, it was more likely to be someone from the far right. It was something we felt intuitively, if abstractly. In the last ten years, that feeling has become stronger. The forces at work on the far right connecting Jews to malicious plots to destroy America are starting to have a real-world impact: In Charlottesville, at the Tree of Life synagogue shooting in Pittsburgh, at the synagogue in Poway. The man who murdered eleven Jews in Pittsburgh did so because he had learned that the Tree of Life congregation had committed to helping refugees through HIAS (Hebrew Immigrant Aid Society), a Jewish-American nonprofit that since its founding in 1881 has helped immigrants and refugees arrive and settle in the United States. The event, however, that most opened my eyes to the danger of right-wing antisemitism and shook my soul was one that I lived through myself: January 6, 2021.

For me, January 6—and the day leading up to it—were, to borrow from Charles Dickens, the best of times and the worst of times. January 5 was the date of two runoff elections in Georgia.

The state's election rules allow for a runoff if neither candidate captures more than 50 percent in the main November election. Democrats and Independents had, at that point, forty-eight Senate seats and Republicans had fifty—meaning that if, somehow, both Democratic candidates in Georgia could win their runoff election, the Senate would be dead-even at fifty. Our Constitution imagined such a scenario, making the vice president of the United States a Constitutional officer of the Senate, able to cast the tie-breaking vote. Because Joe Biden had won the presidency and Kamala Harris was the vice president elect, two wins in Georgia would mean that Democrats would run the United States Senate, and I would become the Senate Majority Leader.

I stayed up all night on January 5 as the results were trickling in from the rural counties outside of Atlanta. By around four in the morning, the networks had projected that our candidates, Raphael Warnock, a Black pastor, and Jon Ossoff, a Jew, would win—two firsts for Georgia, an amazing moment for America. The races were not officially called yet, but in that moment, alone in my chair at home in Brooklyn in front of the television at four in the morning, I felt an indescribable feeling of satisfaction—the kind that you may experience only a few times in your life. It was the joy of achieving my dream, the one I held closest and deepest in my heart, the one I carried with me through nearly four decades in politics. It was the dream of a slightly crazy twenty-three-year-old Jewish kid who turned down a lucrative job at a fancy law firm to run for New York State Assembly against the wishes of his own mother and won, despite the fact that she told all of her friends not to vote for me so, as she said, I would get the idea of being an elected official "out of my big thick skull." Forty-seven years later, I was about to become the first Jewish Senate Majority Leader, and in fact, the highest-ranking Jewish elected official in American history.

I finally got to bed as the sun was rising. After a few hours of restless sleep, I woke up to drive to Washington. I got there a little after noon on January 6 for the counting of the Electoral College ballots by a joint session of Congress and Senate. At around 1 p.m., it all began. The results of Alabama and Alaska were read aloud, along with the winner of the state and the corresponding number of electoral college votes. Arizona's results were announced next, but Congressman Paul Gosar and Senator Ted Cruz objected. And so, fifteen minutes into the process, the joint session was adjourned to allow each chamber to debate and vote on the objection. The senators and I moved to the Senate chamber. I was starting to feel pretty good. I knew that even if Republicans objected a few more times on behalf of President Trump's false claims regarding election fraud, those objections had no merit and would be shot down. I was the putative Majority Leader. Joe Biden was about to be certified as the next president. My colleagues were catching my eyes in between votes, giving thumbs-up or glancing smiles of congratulations.

And then I felt a sharp tug on my shirt collar.

The Senate chamber doesn't have any outward-facing windows. It's set inside the north wing of the Capitol and is mostly shrouded from the sights and sounds of the outside world. So we had not heard the din outside, growing in volume, of scuffles and shouts and upturned metal barricades and collapsed fencing, the pounding of fists and flagpoles (sharpened into spears) at the doors and windows of the building. I first understood something was wrong when that police officer grabbed me by the collar, an action that was so out of custom. It wasn't being touched that alarmed me. The Senate is not such a formal place. My colleagues would slap me on the back from time to time or grab my elbow to get my attention or say goodbye after a long congressional session. But a yank around the neck—that is rare, and it was jarring.

I looked up at the dais at the front of the Senate chamber. Vice President Mike Pence had been grabbed, too, and was being rushed out. "Senator, you're in danger," I heard. It was a member of my personal security detail, Mike Lanczycki, a half-Polish, half-Portuguese cop from Fall River, Massachusetts, whose composure under pressure might have saved my life that day.

"We gotta get out of here," he said.

We started walking briskly, not yet aware that anyone had made it inside the building. At some point, another police officer joined our party and began walking on the other side of me. Only then did I realize they were flanking me for my protection. We passed through a door that led toward the Capitol's central corridor. That was when we saw a mob of people in front of us, less than thirty feet away in the hallway. "There's the big Jew. Let's get him," one of them said.

I was immediately pulled right back through the door we had just come through. With such a frenzy at that moment, I didn't have time to stop and think. Only later did the thought occur to me: What if one of those rioters had had a gun when they saw us? What if two or three of them had run toward us and blocked the door? Who knows what would have happened. But we made it out unscathed. Along with the rest of the congressional leadership, we were taken away to a secure location, undisclosed to us until we arrived.

It was there that the four leaders—Nancy Pelosi, Kevin McCarthy, Mitch McConnell, and myself—were held for the next several hours. We watched the mayhem unfold on a small television in the corner. Everyone was shocked, shaken, but also angry. All four of us were calling various security services: the Maryland and Virginia governors to send their National Guards, the DC mayor for additional Metropolitan Police units, the Pentagon to deploy the DC National Guard; trying to get help to the Capitol Police to manage the mob, arrest the insurrectionists, and clear the building. We were focused on pleading with Trump administration officials to get the president to call off his supporters by tweet, statement, or video—anything. I tried desperately to reach the secretary of defense and the attorney general, and whenever I got an official on the phone, I demanded that the call be put through to Trump, to no avail.

In the middle of that chaotic scene, the news came in: The results in Georgia were now official. Both Democrats had won; I had just become the next Majority Leader. As the image flashed on the television screen of a man carrying the Confederate flag, the symbol of disunion, outside the Senate chamber, Mitch McConnell turned to me and offered his succinct but sincere congratulations. I told him, just as sincerely, "Let's try to work together." It was the best of times and the worst of times.

Around six in the early evening, we got word that the building had been mostly cleared. The room went silent for a moment—and I don't remember who spoke up first—but the four of us decided, immediately and unanimously, to go back to the Hill, resume our work, and finish counting the electoral ballots. Law enforcement officials cautioned against it: There might be a few stragglers they had missed. A more potent concern was the possibility that someone might have left a bomb or chemical agent in the building. The feeling in the room was unchanged. Everyone was adamant. We were going back. We were determined not to let a few rioters hijack our government. It will go down in history as a profound moment of bipartisan statesmanship.

In that moment, I believed something had shifted in my Republican colleagues. The threat to their safety, the safety of their staff and colleagues, and the safety of our democracy felt like a final straw. They seemed furious with President Trump for inciting the riot, and especially his unwillingness to help get it under control, his disregard for the scenes of utter mayhem on Capitol Hill and for the safety of his own vice president. It created a sense of patriotism, duty, and solidarity in that room, which made me believe we could overcome the immense political divisions that President Trump had so gleefully cultivated and exploited. It gave me a degree of hope in a very bleak time.

That feeling wasn't to last. Only a few weeks later, Kevin McCarthy would decamp to Mar-a-Lago to patch things up with Trump after the House had delivered its articles of impeachment to the Senate. In the Senate, Mitch McConnell had some harsh words for President Trump in the days after the insurrection; but he ultimately led most of his Republican colleagues to acquit him, allowing him to run for office once again.

On the night of January 6, we returned to the House and Senate chambers. We resumed certifying Joe Biden's presidential victory. In my remarks that evening, I paid tribute to the courage of the Capitol Police officers, praised the decision to get back to work, and tried to offer some sense of hope about the strength of American democracy, despite the display we had just witnessed. It was my first speech as the impending Majority Leader. We committed to finish the entire count that night; it took us until four in the morning. Months later, one of my Democratic colleagues framed an original record of the final vote that day, the certification of all fifty states that made Joe Biden the president, signed by my fellow senators. It hangs in my office today. To me, it has always been a reminder of the need to fight back, to meet the agents of chaos with conviction, strength, and resolve.

Audio recordings and video footage from that day came out slowly over the course of the following few months, and they were included as evidence in Donald Trump's second impeachment trial and the House's select committee investigation of the January 6 attack on the US Capitol. More footage was included in a documentary produced by Speaker Pelosi's daughter, Alexandra. So I don't remember exactly when I first came across all the instances of antisemitism on January 6, but there were several, a reminder that while the main driver of the riots wasn't antisemitism, it always seems to travel in extreme right-wing circles. Rioters were seen to have made the Nazi salute outside the building, swastikas were displayed on flags and other totems, stickers were placed on clothing that identified some of the rioters as members of the NSC, or Nationalist Social Club, a reference to the Nazi Party. One insurrectionist wore a T-shirt with the alphanumeric slogan 6MWE—"Six Million Wasn't Enough." Another made it inside the Capitol wearing a black sweatshirt stamped with the words CAMP AUSCHWITZ above a skull and crossbones and the text WORK BRINGS FREEDOM, a rough translation of the German phrase welded above the entrance to the death camps. The back of the shirt said STAFF. I thought immediately of those twenty-two thousand American Nazis at Madison Square Garden. If they were alive today, I knew they'd be the kind of people to storm the Capitol.

For me and for many others, January 6 was a searing reminder of the consequences of political extremism, of what happens when conspiracy theories, ultranationalism, and bigotry are allowed to flourish and given a direction and a target. In the immediate aftermath of the insurrection, the country was focused on the implications for our political system and the health of our democracy, as it should have been. But it's also true that the same forces that inspired the rioters on January 6 are the ones that fuel antisemitism. It was not an antisemitic event in its impetus, but it was, in the words of the vice president of the ADL's Center on Extremism, "the latest explicit example of how [antisemitism] is part of what animates the narratives of extremists in this country." So long as a hard-edged combative nationalism in America is allowed to rise, and the denigration of decency in public life is allowed to continue, so long as conspiracy theories circulate, and bigotry is normalized, the threat of violent, right-wing antisemitism will remain all too high.

A year and a half after January 6, I attended a ceremony in Buffalo, New York, to mourn ten lives—all of them Black— taken by an eighteen-year-old white nationalist in a shooting at a grocery store. He believed in the great replacement theory, that Jews were using nonwhite people to destroy Gentile white societies.

EVEN AFTER LEARNING about these incidents, some will say the fears many Jews have about antisemitism on the right are exaggerated. After all, neo-Nazis are not a large movement in America. The present-day Klan is on the fringe. The lone gunman is someone to be afraid of, but he's still just an isolated person. But the true danger lurks not in those individuals but in the potency of totalizing ideas, and the possibility that isolated moments of extreme anti-Jewish hatred will someday engender movements.

Hard-right conspiracy theories that place Jews at the center of a global plot to destroy America and the West are growing in both stature and following. QAnon, once a laughable but overtly antisemitic internet theory propagated by a few wackos, has seeped into the brains of some Republican representatives. The number of mainstream conservatives who call it out is not nearly large enough. The great replacement theory, a less overtly antisemitic ideology but one that still contains incredibly dangerous antisemitic undertones, has had even greater success traveling toward the middle. Republican senators, presidential candidates, and everyday conservative columnists and commentators on Fox News and other right-wing news networks dabble in its murky waters. Many of those talking heads use it for political purposes, to express anti-immigration views or to blame Democrats for society's problems, neither of which is expressly antisemitic. But resting at the core of great replacement theory is a question: Who is responsible for the replacing? Is it George Soros or some other cabal of Jewish international bankers? Therein lies an antisemitic time bomb, and the great replacement theory all too often ensnares Jews in its dragnet of conspiracy. If it becomes even more mainstream, it's a conspiracy that can implant a dangerous antisemitism in American society.

That's what we Jews truly fear. History has taught us that the worst chapters for Jews in modern society begin when far-right movements that contain elements of antisemitism are allowed to bloom into something far more virulent and violent. Antisemitic feelings on the right may be less visible to the average American than those coming from the left. But they reflect deep forces—powerful and arcane.

Antisemitism itself is not, and has never been, an invention of the right. It long predates any modern conception of right or left and transcends any particular political point of view. What's important to understand is why certain ideological movements on the right latch on to antisemitism and—inadvertently or by design—help spread it. What troubles Jews about the current state of the American right is that many of the concepts that have proven most susceptible to antisemitic thinking in history are present today: a reemergence of ethnonationalism, a resentment of cultural elites, an Us vs. Them mentality, and conspiratorial thinking.

That is why it is not the isolated gunman we fear most, as fearful as that person may be. More than the man with his finger on the trigger, we fear the ideas that would drive him to pull it. The shootings in Pittsburgh and Poway are indicative of the fact that antisemitism has started to penetrate the American consciousness. Those ideas are the ones that must be called out, rebutted, put down. And it isn't happening enough. Too many are tolerated or left unchallenged, particularly by those leaders on the right who can more effectively combat them than those of us on the left.

Our fears grow in that silence. If antisemitism is allowed to gain a permanent foothold on the radical right—if it is ignored and allowed to fester—the potential exists for a right-leaning political party or leader to see antisemitism as a useful tactic to galvanize support and whip up populist fervor. If such a leader or party were to win an election or gain a substantial following in Congress, their expression of antisemitism could become further normalized in society. That's when widespread bigotry and even mass violence against Jews become possible.

I would say to my friends on the right: We know you don't harbor these ideas and probably abhor them, so please shout them down. We need you to do more to put out the fire of antisemitism that is spreading around the edges of your political camp. Just as many on the right justifiably feel that Democrats have an obligation to shout down antisemitism on the left, Republicans have an obligation to shout down antisemitism coming from the right. There has been too much silence on the issue by the right in general, and by conservative officeholders in particular. That must change.

CHAPTER 7

ANTISEMITISM ON THE LEFT

As a lifelong Democrat who has always worked alongside the progressive movement, watching antisemitism grow in some parts of the American left has been extremely painful. Truthfully, it's much harder to grapple with than antisemitism on the right. Jews know that far-right movements tend to cast us as villains. We expect it, and we never really had close relationships with the kind of antisemites whose hatred for Jews is overt. We didn't share any of their values or ideals, and we knew we would have to fight them. But most Jews have always had a natural affinity for the American left. Throughout American history, mainstream Jewish-Americans made up a core of most liberal coalitions. Liberals and progressives have been our fellow travelers, our partners, our political allies, our friends. And so, when Jewish-Americans have seen antisemitism emerging from these corners, we have struggled to treat it fairly and directly—not to overreact, for instance, by claiming that all anti-Israel rhetoric is antisemitic, which of course it isn't. But we also understand that when protest rhetoric and actions go overboard—when they slip and bleed into antisemitism in language or theme—it is dangerous and even leads to violence against Jews.

In trying to come to terms with recent events, especially the protests over the war in Gaza, I found myself thinking back to a chapter in my life also defined by protest—my history as a student leader in the late 1960s and early 1970s. It is not a story about antisemitism, but it is about many of the same feelings that I and other Jews have right now: feelings of tension with our political friends and allies, and frustration at the tactics that some have adopted. I believe it contains, too, lessons for our current moment about the consequences of failing to keep a lid on the boiling anger of protest movements, even when the anger itself is deeply felt. When does protest go too far? When does it become counterproductive? My personal experience with campus protest has shaped my own answers to those questions.

IN 1967, THE son of an exterminator (yours truly) got into Harvard, a rarity. Like many things in life, it was the combination of hard work and good luck. I was a so-so basketball player with good grades—a decent-enough college applicant—but it was one of my extracurricular activities that helped seal the deal. I had to get a job when I was fourteen, like many of my friends did to help support our families. I tore the first notice I saw from the bulletin board at school. A math teacher at Madison High School was starting a new business and looking for a part-time clerical worker to run a mimeograph machine, a somewhat medieval, hand-cranked variety of copying that preceded Xerox. (The ink from the machine was the best legal high you could get. I tell younger people that if we still had mimeographs, we wouldn't need to legalize marijuana.) I got the job.

What was this new business? The teacher had had a brilliant idea: He was going to help students prepare and get higher scores on the SATs. What was his name? Stanley Kaplan. Twenty years later, he sold the business to the *Washington Post* for $45 million. On nights, holidays, and weekends, I stood in a windowless, three-by-three-foot room, reeling out copies. By reading the preparatory materials over and over and over again as the machine went round and round and round, I got 800s on my SATs. I might have been the first to prove the test was not about aptitude but achievement. And so, a middle-class Jewish kid from Brooklyn snuck into Harvard.

When I arrived on campus, my exceptionally average basketball skills weren't enough to get me past the first tryout for the freshman team. The coach sent me home without ever watching me touch a ball—they weren't welcoming this six-foot-one forward to the team. I was distraught, but again, fate smiled on me. The same night I got cut, I got a knock on my door. Again, it was bashert—destiny. Standing there was a fellow student who asked if I wanted to join the Harvard Young Democrats. They were looking for volunteers to work on the campaign of Eugene McCarthy, a senator from Minnesota who was running against Lyndon B. Johnson in the New Hampshire primary on the basis that America should not be in a war in Vietnam. I didn't have a political bone in my body, but I hated that goddamn war. At the time, if you didn't go to college, you could be drafted right out of high school. I'd hear about my former classmates, eighteen or nineteen years old, drafted straight out of school and dead within ten months in a jungle ten thousand miles away.

So I volunteered for the campaign. The next day, I got on a bus with a whole bunch of kids from the Boston area, and we went up to New Hampshire to campaign for McCarthy. I loved it. It was like sports. As a group, we devised our own leaflets, divided up neighborhoods, brainstormed slogans: all working as a team. I fell into politics headfirst.

Even though Eugene McCarthy didn't end up winning the primary, he got so close that a few weeks later President Johnson announced that he would withdraw from the race. I was amazed and awed. A rag-tag bunch of students and other nobodies helped topple the most powerful man in the world. I thought to myself: *What a system! I want to dedicate my life to this.* Over the following three years, I spent my time working for candidates who were against the war, organizing marches, peacefully protesting and picketing. (Nowadays, I like to tell the more peaceful protesters who regularly picket my home on many different issues that I understand what they are doing. I say: If I was your age, I would probably be picketing against something I thought was an injustice, too.)

Two of the candidates I found myself working for were unknown but principled moderates: Romano Mazzoli and David Obey, Democrats running for Congress in rather conservative districts in Kentucky and Wisconsin, respectively. They were both passionately against the war and ran for elected office because they believed the best way to make an impact was to change things from the inside. Twenty years later I would be serving with them in Congress.

If a bunch of kids could topple LBJ, I thought, *surely we could change the system through peaceful protest and electoral politics.* I had decided that the best way to bring about change was to work within the system, whatever its flaws. I recently came across an article I wrote in the *Harvard Independent* in 1971 that perfectly summed up my views: "For bureaucratic power, with all of its inhumanity and inefficiency, is one of the few ways to get larger things done in the world." I still feel that way.

I arrived at Harvard in the fall of 1967, a time when there were still elements of 1950s elite culture on campus. You had to wear a jacket and tie to breakfast, lunch, and dinner. Everyone had short hair, women were only allowed to visit us in our dorm rooms during certain hours, and everyone was required to keep at least one foot on the floor at all times! A lot would change in the years I spent on campus. As freshman year rolled into sophomore year, I experienced one of the most chaotic and politically charged moments in American history. Tastes, attitudes, politics (especially gender politics), haircuts, and attire all quickly evolved. Robert F. Kennedy and Martin Luther King Jr. were assassinated within a few months of each other. And in large part because of the war in Vietnam, emotions ran hot on campus and eventually boiled over.

There were plenty of students who didn't share my view of political engagement. At the time, two of the most active groups on campus were the Students for a Democratic Society, or SDS, and the Progressive Labor Party, or PLP. They had unofficially merged, though it was not a marriage made in heaven. The SDS kids smoked pot, wore bell bottoms, and believed their mission was to heave themselves onto the gears of the machinery to bring it all crashing down. The PLP kids, on the other hand, were more diligent Maoists. They shunned drugs, and in an era of long hairdos, kept their hair short. They wore old-fashioned clothes so that they could go into factories, mingle with the workers, and "organize the white working class." In my opinion and in the opinion of many of my classmates at Harvard, the PLP-SDS kids were too radical. They were self-important, maximalist, and when you disagreed with them, their first instinct was not to give you reasons why they thought they were right and you were wrong, it was to dismiss you and call you a traitor to the cause. They felt that they were the ultimate arbiters of Truth and Right, and it gave them permission to be arrogant and nasty. I'd hear stories of them harassing the more politically moderate students on campus. They went so far as to mercilessly taunt some of the moderate Black student leaders for being sellouts or Uncle Toms—really ugly stuff. I was totally appalled by their demeanor and by their methods. They believed not in persuasion but coercion: occupy a building, block a street, camp out in the student union or library. Like many of us, they felt the Vietnam War was totally immoral, but the difference was that the PLP-SDS felt it gave them license to do anything, no matter how cruel or harsh.

It all came to a head in the spring of 1969. The prior year had been the deadliest one for American soldiers in Vietnam, not to speak of the two hundred thousand dead Vietnamese. The SDS had lost patience with the Harvard administration over refusing to remove ROTC from campus (many of us opposed having ROTC programs on campus because it aided the war effort), among other issues, and wanted to take bold action to show their opposition. On the afternoon of April 9, a group of about one hundred students forced their way into University Hall, one of the main administrative buildings, kicked out the deans, and began rifling through files. The sit-in lasted overnight, and the number of student protesters, inside and outside the Hall, swelled to five hundred as the hours went by.

I, along with a group of moderate student leaders, pleaded with the university not to call in the police—that was surely what the SDS wanted, a confrontation. Instead, we suggested that Harvard hold a gathering at Soldiers Field the next day, where a vote could be taken to chart a path forward. Anyone from Harvard could go—student, professor, janitor—and vote on two questions. Should ROTC leave campus? And should SDS end their occupation of University Hall? We assured the administration that more than 90 percent of the student body would say yes to both questions, and if the university endorsed the results, Harvard could potentially end the standoff without confrontation. The administration gave us the green light. We ran back to the offices of the Harvard Young Dems and started printing off the ballot questions on the mimeo machines that we owned.

Just before sunrise, I got a call from one of the deans. The administration had changed its mind. There would be no ballot, no vote, no peaceful arbitration. The university had called in the cops. More than four hundred police officers from Somerville, Cambridge, and Boston—born and bred to hate the "Hahvies"— took position outside University Hall, armed with riot shields and Mace. A few minutes after 5 a.m., the police stormed the building, and forcibly removed all the students in a brief but violent clash. Between 250 and 300 arrests were made, and around 75 students and police officers suffered injuries. I saw one cop bash a woman across the back of her head with his nightstick;

her body slumped to the ground and her camera along with it. She was my friend's girlfriend, only there to take pictures.

I did not agree with the SDS and their occupation of the Hall, but I was sufficiently pissed off at the administration that I joined a handful of other moderate student leaders in supporting a general strike on campus. CONFRONTATION IN HARVARD YARD blared the headline on the cover of the April 25, 1969, issue of *Life* magazine, below which you can find a picture of me, facing away from camera, wearing a head of bushy hair and a white T-shirt spray-painted with the stencil of a raised red fist and the word STRIKE. (My friends at the time said that I had an "Isro," the Jewish equivalent of an Afro. Nowadays people call it a Jewfro.) The strike lasted eight days and included two mass meetings at Soldiers Field that yielded some minor policy changes at our university.

Looking back, the spring of 1969 determined how I came to understand and relate to the art of politics, protest, and left-leaning movements. I spent my time picketing and protesting the war, and I probably agreed with some of my more radical classmates on a handful of issues. But I saw how their zeal and fury led them to be not only demeaning to other students but disruptive, which was ultimately counterproductive. They turned too many people off. During my sophomore year, despite all the campus protests and building opposition to the war, Nixon defeated Humphrey (the moderate Democratic candidate) in the election. Some commentators have argued that Nixon won the presidency not because most voters were for the war—they were not—but because they were even angrier at the behavior of some of the protesters, especially after seeing the televised images from the streets of Chicago during the

Democratic Convention. Nixon, the "law and order" candidate, took full advantage.

That semester was one of turmoil, not only on campus but in my own head. One night I was so aggravated that I couldn't sleep. The division, anger, and name-calling on campus deeply troubled me. Instead of lying there with my eyes open, staring at the ceiling, I decided to get up and go for a walk around midnight. I found myself heading south from Harvard's campus, away from the dingy basement bars and burger joints of Harvard Square toward the peaceful banks of the Charles River, which separates the city of Boston from Cambridge. Everything was still and quiet for what felt like the first time in months. I was able to reflect on so much that had happened. The deafness of the administration and the resulting violence on campus bothered me a great deal. What bothered me almost as much was the behavior of the small but vocal minority of my friends and peers who I felt had precipitated the crisis. I knew these kids. They were in my dorm. I knew they hated the war and felt a burning passion to do something real about it. But why were they going way over the line, resorting to spite and intimidation? Why were they bullying those of us who agreed with them but just wanted to make a difference in a peaceful way? They reminded me of Rosa Luxemburg, a Polish-German socialist revolutionary I had studied in history class, and who my professor drolly remarked appeared to have loved humanity in the abstract but looked down on almost every human she met. Those quandaries rolled over and over in my mind.

You can walk along the Charles for a good while, past Fenway and Back Bay and toward the West End, before you have to loop around back toward Cambridge. As my footfalls piled up, I began to come to a resolution. I thought to myself: *Chuck, if you focus mainly on the bad stuff, both in people and in groups, you will end up hating everything and everyone. You'll be an unhappy person and it will be an unhappy world. The better thing you can do is look for the good in people and try to meet them there.*

A few of my peers were angry, and I could see why. Some of them were behaving badly, but at least they were trying to do some good, even if, in my opinion, they were going about it in the wrong way. Many of these kids came from enormous privilege. They didn't have to be protesting the war. Like so many of their well-to-do friends, they could have been driving in fancy cars to the junior colleges to try to pick up girls for one-night stands. Instead, they were trying to end the war—albeit in a counterproductive manner.

I knew, though, that I was never going to be on the side of the radicals. I was going to take my own path and try to work through the system and get results, even if it meant compromise and concession from time to time. I was going to try to look for the good in everyone, a lesson that has stayed with me throughout my life. I was going to at least try to understand where people were coming from. And even if I failed and they shut me down and some of them told me I was a sellout, I would try to convince them to seek progress with me on the issues we both cared about. It was more of a human principle and less of a political one, but after a long and fraught year, it brought me a sense of peace.

MY EXPERIENCES OF antiwar campus activism in the late 1960s have greatly influenced my feelings about the protests against

Israel and how these relate to antisemitism. Protests at Harvard returned, full flourish, this past year. I remember vividly a photo I saw in the *Wall Street Journal*: a group of students sitting at long desks inside a packed room in a building on campus. They were wearing keffiyehs, traditional Palestinian scarves, and the same sign was affixed to all their laptops: NO NORMALCY DURING GENOCIDE. JUSTICE FOR PALESTINE. They were occupying the Reading Room of Widener Library, the main library at Harvard, surely discomfiting every student who was there to study. As a student at Harvard from 1967 to 1974, through undergraduate lessons and law school, I studied at Widener all the time. I loved its quiet majesty and had treasured the place as a penultimate temple of learning and debate.

The photo was from the winter of 2023, a few months after the October 7 attacks and the beginning of the war in Gaza. The conflict touched an extremely sensitive nerve in America, drawing protests and counterprotests in cities and in college towns. Harvard's University Hall had again been occupied, as were buildings on other campuses; students set up encampments in quads and open spaces, and demanded that their universities' endowments be divested from Israeli companies; sympathetic professors led Palestine solidarity teach-ins. The protesters argued that since America is Israel's strongest ally, and because America provides Israel aid and weaponry, America itself was complicit in the war and the devastation in Gaza, both human and material. The protesters demanded that the United States pressure Israel to commit to an immediate and permanent ceasefire, that the United States condition its military aid on Israel's adherence to international and American law.

I could hear what they were saying, and while I disagreed

with their conclusions, I empathized with the urgent need for less human suffering. But what deeply alarmed me, apart from the stridency of the messaging about Israel committing and America enabling what they consider "genocide," was how some of the slogans at the protests, voiced by some students and by outside agitators, were becoming indistinguishable from the vilest antisemitic screeds. The day after the Widener Library sit-in, a woman screamed at a group of Jews and non-Jews gathered on campus for an outdoor candle-lighting ceremony for Hanukkah that the Holocaust was fake. The Hanukkah menorah that's been kindled and displayed on Harvard Yard during the winter holiday for nearly twenty-five years had to be taken indoors each night to protect it from vandalism.

The menorah has been a symbol of Judaism for thousands of years, long before the creation of the modern State of Israel. Hanukkah is a Jewish religious holiday meant to celebrate the strength and resilience of our people, no matter where they reside. For that reason, Jews are instructed not only to light the menorah but to place it on our homes' windowsills for the eight nights of Hanukkah so everyone can see that we are proud to be Jewish. At one of the world's most prestigious universities— supposed to be a paradigm of free speech—the expression of Jewish pride was not safe at night.

The events at Harvard struck close to home. To think that some could let fury at a war being fought on foreign soils spill over into the abuse of Jews and outright antisemitism at home filled me with dismay and even anger. The events in Cambridge were a microcosm of what was happening in too many places in America. At other colleges, in left-leaning social justice movements and organizations, and eventually rippling through liberal American media and progressive politics, the war in Gaza became a focal point, the source of much genuine protest, but also, in too many cases, a catalyst for antisemitism. Protest chants on campuses started going far beyond expressions of solidarity with Palestinians. At UCLA, protesters beat a piñata bearing an image of Prime Minister Netanyahu while a woman shouted into a megaphone: "Beat that fucking Jew."

During a particularly fraught period of competing pro-Israel and pro-Palestine demonstrations at Columbia University in the first few weeks after the war began, Jewish students described a climate of intimidation and harassment. A student wearing a yarmulke reported that he was getting a meal in the kosher section of a campus dining hall when another student approached him and said, "Fuck the Jews." In April, just outside the university gates, a protester screamed at Jewish students walking by: "The seventh of October is about to be every day for you." The following night, Jewish students exiting the university were told to "go back to Poland."

In late May, Columbia hosted a panel discussion called "Jewish Life on Campus: Past, Present and Future." Sitting in the audience, three university administrators, including the dean of undergraduate student life and the associate dean for student and family support, sent each other text messages in which they mocked the panelists for showing concern for Columbia's Jewish students. "Comes from such a place of privilege," one wrote, "hard to hear the 'woe is me.'" When an alumna in the audience broke down in tears while sharing her daughter's nervousness as a Jewish student on campus, another administrator wrote, "Amazing what $$$$ can do." The three deans were properly removed from their posts, and later resigned.

Unfortunately, apart from those Columbia administrators and a few other egregious examples, there was a widespread failure to discipline both faculty and students who engaged in overtly antisemitic activities and those that made Jewish students feel unsafe on campus. General chants and even threats aimed at Jews, whether the Jewish students were pro-Israel or not, were rarely shouted down or categorized as hate speech. Specific instances of antisemitic harassment against Jewish students were frequently ignored due to a "lack of sufficient information," according to many reports. To me, many college administrations were too slow to react to antisemitism in their own backyards, and even more hesitant to take disciplinary action against offenders. I've raised my voice many times, publicly and privately, to push administrations to do much more to stop antisemitism from spreading on America's campuses. While many feared that antisemitism would get worse when schools opened in the fall of 2024, fortunately, there have been fewer instances than in the previous school year, which many reports attribute to the fact that administrations are finally taking disciplinary action against antisemitic and disruptive protests that cross the line. This decline is to be welcomed, but it is no reason for college administrations to relax—it could spring back up at any time.

FOR JEWISH-AMERICANS, CONCERN has been growing that the rise of antisemitism is not being taken seriously enough and, at times, is even stoked by the political left; that aspects of the debate over the proportionality of Israel's military response to the Hamas attacks have crossed over into a much darker place;

that Jewish people are being targeted simply for being Jewish, for reasons that have nothing to do with Israel.

Many recent examples are quite easy to identify as antisemitism, whether the culprit belongs to the left, the right, or neither:

- Vandalizing or threatening synagogues or Jewish community centers.
- Vandalizing or boycotting Jewish businesses and delis.
- Harassing Jewish educators, such as emailing a high school teacher: "All Jews need to be exterminated."
- Etching swastikas into desks at a high school and painting graffiti on the walls reading JEWS NOT WELCOME.
- Punching someone who is wearing a yarmulke and dousing him with pepper spray, shouting "Dirty Jew. Filthy Jew, Fuck Israel. Hamas is going to kill you."

These are not isolated or one-time incidents; they occur all too frequently and in many parts of the country. There can be no question that these are examples of antisemitism.

Others, while very troubling, may be a bit more difficult to parse. The terms "Zionism" and "Zionist," for example, have a rich history and have been the subject of hefty scholarship but are now used by some as a way to castigate Jews. People who mean to say "you dirty Jew," now say "you dirty Zionist."

Zionism originated as a nationalist movement in late-nineteenth-century Europe that aimed to establish a state for

Jews in their ancestral homeland, the land of Israel. Its derivative, "Zionist," refers to those who support Israel's right to exist
as a Jewish homeland. The term "Zionist" can be appropriately
used in the context of a reasoned argument. But it can also be,
and often has been, divorced from its meaning and used as an
accusation, a slur, a complete substitute for the word "Jew."

When does other criticism of Israel coming from the left
slide over into antisemitism, and why do many Jews view some
pro-Palestinian slogans as antisemitic but not others? What
ideas are causing some antiwar protesters to feel that because
of events in the Middle East, any Jew is a valid target of harassment and delegitimization?

In a sense, these questions are more wrenching to most Jewish-
Americans than questions about antisemitism on the far right,
which is more likely to be explicit. Jews understand intuitively that
neo-Nazis and Proud Boys and Klansmen will be antisemitic. But
a handful of stalwart progressives? Not that long ago, many of us
had marched together for Black and Brown lives, we stood side by
side against anti-Asian hatred, we protested bigotry against the
LGBTQ community, and we fought for reproductive justice out
of the recognition that injustice against one oppressed group is
injustice against all. But recently, when antisemitic and even violently antisemitic rhetoric appeared at rallies organized by left-
leaning groups, it felt like a much more personal betrayal.

More than that, however, it felt that with the frighten-
ing increase in antisemitism in corners of the political right, a
resurgence of antisemitism on the left presented an immense
danger: that the two could intensify and feed off one another—
pincers that would attack the Jews from both sides—leaving us
with no natural political allies. Alone, once again, against the

world. More than anything, Jewish-Americans are worried, given the twists and turns of history, about where this new left-leaning antisemitism could lead.

As with antisemitism on the right, I found that I needed to look at history to best understand where the recent antisemitism on the American left originated. As out of the blue as these recent displays of antisemitism on campus can feel, and as jarring as its presence is in such liberal environs, hatred and prejudice against Jews has had roots in left-wing movements over the past two centuries.

Many scholars have argued that the ideas that animate left-wing antisemitism were present in Karl Marx's 1844 essay "On the Jewish Question," which linked Judaism with the cult of money and argued that human emancipation from capitalism could not occur unless Jews were emancipated from Judaism itself. "What is the worldly religion of the Jew? *Huckstering*. What is his worldly God? *Money*," he wrote. While some of Marx's writings show more sympathy for the plight of the Jewish people, much of the antisemitism witnessed in Communist states derived from his negative strain of thought: that Jews represent a minority with a special interest (namely, capitalism) that undermines the collective spirit and aspirations of equality under communism. The political leadership of the Soviet Union took it to heart. Joseph Stalin, especially, relied upon antisemitism to consolidate his power and then turned the apparatus of the state against Soviet Jewry, labeling them spies and traitors to the revolution.

Many tomes have been devoted to the trauma of the Jews under the fierce anti-Zionism of Stalinist Russia and the latent antisemitism of the European far left, but for the purposes of an American observer, it is important to understand the argument at the core of Marx's observation, which was later twisted and applied savagely by communist and socialist apparatchiks. Essentially, Marx, whose Jewish parents had converted and baptized their children in the Lutheran Church, believed that the Jewish religion—and Jewish people who wanted to retain an attachment to their culture and traditions—was an obstacle to progressive social and economic progress.

Antisemitism in leftist and socialist circles has survived well into the twenty-first century. An example that I imagine many Americans are familiar with pertains to the UK Labour Party under Jeremy Corbyn's leadership. In 2020, a report by an independent watchdog group found that Labour under Corbyn had suffered from "serious failings" of leadership "in addressing antisemitism and had an inadequate process for handling antisemitism complaints." It found evidence that complaints about grossly antisemitic comments and images (including a mural of hook-nosed Jewish bankers) were ignored, and members who'd made the complaints were harassed. Corbyn, a self-described socialist, was suspended and later booted out of the party, in part for playing down the report's conclusions.

The American left, by contrast, has long been welcoming to Jews, and in turn, Jewish-Americans have played a leading role in voicing and shaping the concerns and priorities of the left. In a certain sense, the Jews didn't have a choice. The right wing in America in the early part of the twentieth century was isolationist, anti-immigrant, elitist, and antisemitic—it did not welcome the poor Yiddish-speaking Jewish immigrants arriving bedraggled from Eastern Europe upon its shores. But more

ANTISEMITISM ON THE LEFT

important, Jewish liturgy and teachings from the Old World tended to dovetail with liberal or progressive causes in the new one. Tzedakah, or charity, was a great mitzvah, or good deed— not just helping your fellow neighbor but helping the poor. The moral ethos of liberal American synagogues was embodied by the concept of Tikkun Olam, repairing the world. Our religious holidays instruct Jews to feel and fight not only our own oppression but the oppression of others. So when Jews came to America, that was exactly what many of them did.

Just like Jewish activists played a leading role in the American labor movement to fight for the rights of the working class, they joined with African-American leaders like W. E. B. Du Bois and Ida B. Wells to found the NAACP in 1909 to fight for racial equality. Rabbi Abraham Joshua Heschel, one of the leading rabbis of his day, marched alongside Reverend Martin Luther King Jr. and a young John Lewis in Selma in March 1965. The summer prior, when I was fourteen years old and the civil rights movement was at its peak, I remember my parents and neighbors talking about Schwerner, Goodman, and Chaney. James Chaney was a young Black man from Mississippi, while Michael Schwerner and Andrew Goodman were Jews from New York City; they were in Jim Crow Mississippi, deep in Dixieland, in June 1964 to help register African-American voters. One day, the three of them drove to a small town to visit the parishioners of a Black church that had been torched to the ground by the Klan. As they were leaving town, they were subject to a "routine" traffic stop. They were held in jail for several nerve-racking hours before being released. I imagine they breathed a long sigh of relief as they left the jailhouse, believing their ordeal was over. But as soon as they began to drive away, they were chased by a lynch mob of Klan members, a mob that included a local sheriff. Schwerner, Chaney, and Goodman were abducted, shot, and buried in an earthen dam. It took the FBI forty-four days to find the bodies. Much later in life, when I became a politician, I used to bump into Goodman's mother, Carolyn, who continued to campaign for social justice in her son's name. The Jewish community of New York has always been proud that, although they paid the ultimate price, Schwerner and Goodman had worked shoulder to shoulder with Chaney for civil rights and voting rights.

For all of these ideological reasons—a belief in minority rights, social justice, and solidarity with other working class and immigrant populations—Jews found a natural home in the Democratic Party, as did many other newly immigrated groups. Since 1932, when FDR first won the presidency, Jewish-Americans have voted for the Democratic candidate by large margins. FDR was revered for getting our country out of the Depression, and Jewish-Americans—many of whom were working-class at the time—benefited from and were strong supporters of the New Deal. FDR would later be seen as a more ambivalent figure for his administration's reluctance to expand immigration quotas so that more Jews could leave Europe and find refuge in America during the Holocaust, and also for its refusal to strafe the train tracks leading to Auschwitz, opting to continue with industrial or military targets.

Another important reason Jews have felt at home in the party was that it was pro-Israel from the start. President Truman was the first world leader to officially recognize the state of Israel, cementing a pro-Israel plank of the Democratic Party that would remain solid, without serious challenge, until recently. I still remember vividly when John F. Kennedy came to Brooklyn for the first time during the 1960 campaign. He held a rally at Dubrow's Cafeteria, a big Jewish deli on Kings Highway. I went with my friends to join the crowd hoping to catch a glimpse of the candidate. On Election Day, I stayed up all night long watching the states on the black-and-white television turn (metaphorically) red or blue.

As I was growing up in the 1950s and '60s, when civil rights and, later, the Vietnam War became the two leading issues of the day, it was sort of accepted in our circles in Brooklyn that Jews would be pro–civil rights and antiwar. It was unusual to meet a Jew who wasn't. It was almost a fact of American political life: The Jews and the left were mishpachah—family.

It wasn't until I arrived at Harvard that I started to notice that certain corners of the progressive movement were hostile to Israel. While opposition to the Vietnam War was widespread on campus, some of my classmates who were part of the SDS or inspired by the Black Power movement, belonged to the "New Left"—as it was called—and they had strong views on the Arab-Israeli conflict, which were just as likely to be anti-Israel as pro-Israel. I did not perceive it as stemming from latent antisemitism, and they certainly were not antisemitic in their interactions with Jewish classmates, but it was the first time I sensed a friction within the left wing of the Democratic Party between anti-Zionists and largely Zionist Jewish-Americans. When Abba Eban, the very articulate Israeli foreign minister, visited our campus in 1970, a group of SDS activists protested his appearance by hanging a banner saying: FIGHT ZIONIST IMPERIALISM.

At the time, it confused and upset me. Israel in that era was far from the powerhouse it is today. It was still a young country, a fledgling democracy surrounded by Arab states that we feared wanted to drive it into the sea. Israel was also associated with left-wing politics. Left-leaning political parties had been in charge ever since independence. Socialist kibbutzim, small communal enclaves, dotted the landscape. So why were there all these leftist opponents of Israel in those days? For one, it was a reaction to the Six-Day War in 1967. Both Egypt and Israel contend that the other nation started the hostilities, but the reaction stemmed from the outcome: Israel defeated the armies of three Arab states (Egypt, Jordan, and Syria) and captured the Gaza Strip, the West Bank, East Jerusalem, the Sinai Peninsula, and the Golan Heights. For the first time, Israel controlled territory beyond its own borders; more than one million Palestinians were now under Israeli rule. Another specific reason for the anti-Zionist turn, as the history professor Michael Fischbach elucidates in the *Journal of Palestine Studies*, relates to Black liberation groups that were part of the New Left: "Because of their overt transnational solidarity with oppressed peoples of color around the world, they naturally embraced the Palestinians as an example of just such a people. They not only identified with them but also saw their own struggle and that of the Arabs in the Middle East as one and the same: a struggle against racialized U.S. imperialism." In truth, however, the vast majority of Israelis at the time were not of Ashkenazi descent, but rather Mizrahi or Sephardic—Middle-Eastern Jews who moved from Iraq, Iran, Turkey, Syria, Jordan, and Morocco in 1948, when Israel was created and Jews were expelled or compelled to leave Arab countries.

Still, there was virtually no antisemitism present in the

antiwar protests I witnessed in college. In seminars and casual conversations, I thought at times that a few of my classmates didn't understand the history of the Jewish people or why having a Jewish homeland was so important to so many Jews, but I don't remember any violence or verbal abuse directed at Jews for supporting Israel or just for being Jewish. But looking back today, I realize that a few signs of future left-wing antipathy toward Israel were present more than fifty years ago, and it was intimately related to conceptions of race and oppression.

OVER THE NEXT half century, as antisemitism throughout American society faded into the background and many Jewish-Americans rose into upper echelons of society, I hardly detected any inkling of antisemitism in leftward movements or in politics. Just as the right had a few cranks and zealots, the far left has had a few marginal figures such as Louis Farrakhan, the Nation of Islam leader who habitually accused Jews of controlling the levers of world power. But then, just as Jews noticed a rekindling of antisemitism on the right in the wake of the financial crisis, we started to see a few signs that the left—our natural home for so many years—was no longer immune to the poison. Again, it was around 2008, the same year the ADL, Franklin Foer, and others have identified as a turning point for rising antisemitism in the twenty-first century.

What was happening on the left at that time? I, for one, started becoming aware of a noticeable shift in focus. While the election of Barack Obama to the presidency evoked a racist panic and caused many on the right to turn to the likes of the Tea Party, not to mention antisemitic conspiracizing, the financial crisis caused many on the left to deepen their existing distrust of financial institutions and financiers, the banking system and bankers, and politicians who were seen as protecting those special interests. None of those thoughts are inherently antisemitic, but they do intersect with historical stereotypes about Jews and finance. One antisemitic conspiracy theory floating around on the internet in the fall of 2008 alleged that Lehman Brothers and other investment banks secretly transferred $400 billion to Israeli banks before going under.

An intellectual framework was also being built on the political left in which Israel wound up on the wrong side of a perceived historical struggle between oppressor and oppressed. This new era of historical re-examination on the left has forced us Americans to grapple with uncomfortable truths in our own history, from the treatment of Native Americans to Japanese-American internment camps to the original sin of slavery and the long shadow of racial prejudice against our Black citizens. Very rightly so. But it also led to a few excesses. To some, looking at the world through the lens of oppression became the only lens that mattered. And in this new world order, because some Jewish people have done exceedingly well in America, because Israel has grown only more powerful over the last several decades, it could appear that Jews have become strong enough to singlehandedly overcome prejudice and bigotry, that in fact we now—to quote the language of some—are the "oppressors." Our own (rather dense) history of being oppressed and persecuted is no longer deemed relevant to the radical fringe. This ideological framework is particularly damaging when young people who are not Jewish are exposed to it, because they tend to be less aware of the long history of antisemitism. And even among Jewish young people, it can sometimes lead to excessive guilt, and the urge to exculpate themselves from feeling responsible.

On college campuses, even before October 7, this new framework led to behavior that clearly steps over the line. In 2020, at the University of Southern California, students demanded the impeachment of the Jewish vice president of their student government over her support for Israel's right to exist as a Jewish state. Does that mean most Jews can't serve in student government? In 2013 and 2014, at Harvard, New York University, and several other universities, student activists slid mock "eviction" and "demolition notices" into the dorm rooms of fellow students, a reference to the rapid expansion of Israeli settlements in Palestinian territories. The target audience clearly was Jewish students, independent of their views on Israel. Surely there are less pernicious ways to register your outrage at another nation's policy than trying to intimidate teenagers at an American university on the basis of their identity. One study by a political scientist at Tufts University in 2024 found that one in five non-Jewish students "wouldn't want to be friends with someone who supports the existence of Israel as a Jewish state." Does that mean they won't be friendly toward any Jewish person until they can prove they don't support Israel? When you consider that eight in ten American Jews consider caring about Israel an essential or important part of what being Jewish means to them, does that mean a significant number of US college students are saying they wouldn't want to be friends with most Jews?

In recent years, we also began to see the splintering of some of the most high-profile progressive groups in America around the issues of antisemitism and Israel. A Jewish activist who'd helped organize the Women's March—one of the largest and most diverse protests in American history, in the wake of Trump's election—was pushed out of the group, she believed, because of her Jewish identity. Three of the group's leaders would eventually step down, one of them over allegations of antisemitism, which included calling Louis Farrakhan the "G.O.A.T.," or "Greatest of All Time," and reportedly saying that Jews needed to confront their own role in racism. Some left-aligned figures in politics and government have also gone too far by using antisemitic tropes while criticizing Israel and its supporters. Representative Ilhan Omar of Minnesota infamously tweeted that support for Israel among Republicans in Congress was "all about the Benjamins, baby" though, to her credit, she subsequently apologized and said, "Anti-Semitism is real and I am grateful for Jewish allies and colleagues who are educating me on the painful history of anti-Semitic tropes."

For the first time in decades, Jewish-Americans were starting to hear and be subject to stereotypes and slander, that Jews were secretly powerful and domineering, that they were racist oppressors, exerting undue influence on politics and media, with our money and privilege. And those things were being said by those we had assumed were our allies on the left.

OCTOBER 7 AND its aftermath was another and the biggest turning point. Deeply troubling were the many examples of antisemitism—the denigration or abuse of Jews for simply being Jewish, not merely criticism of Israel—that started appearing at

protests and in civil society. I will address in greater specificity how the debate around Israel's actions has fostered antisemitism in America. But we must now understand how the recent protest movements on the left have, intentionally or unintentionally, reanimated the specter of antisemitism as well.

While certainly many protesters harbor no ill-intent toward Jews, certain slogans and chants repeated by large groups of protesters have gone way beyond expressing support for the Palestinian cause or principled opposition to Israeli policy. "From the river to the sea," for example, is a slogan that Hamas, a terrorist group, popularized and incorporated into their revised 2017 charter, which calls for "the full and complete liberation"—between the Jordan River and the Mediterranean Sea—"of Palestine." The second part of the chant, "Palestine will be free," may well make it sound aspirational, but the implications of the first half of the slogan cannot be avoided. How will Palestine be liberated from the river to the sea without the end of Israel, without the extermination or forced removal of more than 7 million Jews?

That's basically what the 1988 Hamas founding charter had more straightforwardly called for. It began with a quote by a Muslim Brotherhood leader, "Israel will exist and will continue to exist until Islam will obliterate it, just as it obliterated others before it," and went on to quote a saying attributed to Prophet Muhammad, "The Day of Judgement will not come about until the Muslims fight the Jews [killing the Jews], when the Jew will hide behind stones and trees. The stones and trees will say O Moslems, O Abdullah, there is a Jew behind me, come and kill him." Iran, Hamas's benefactor, believes just as strongly in the destruction of Israel and Jews.

When other minority groups—be they Black, Asian-Americans, LGBTQ, Latino-Americans, Muslim-Americans, recent immigrants from a multitude of backgrounds—hear "dog whistles," expressions of bigotry that they are sensitive to even if the literal meaning is not explicitly racist, community advocates call it out. They say, *Let's not use that expression; it references something hurtful.* A multicultural society tends to join together and condemn the use of those dog whistles. Many words and phrases that were commonly used a few decades ago, even in polite society, are now appropriately no longer in use; they had problematic origins and caused great offense to the particular group. The same standard, I believe, should apply to slogans like "from the river to the sea."

Jews have also been alarmed by even more provocative and intimidating signs at anti-Israel rallies, like those announcing that Palestinians have the right to resist "by any means necessary." Does that mean it is all right to kill all the Jews in Israel? Does that mean that a brutal massacre like October 7 was OK? Does that mean that more massacres of Jews for the sake of Palestinian liberation will be OK? To many of us, that's what "by any means necessary" sounds like. Other frequently used expressions such as "globalize the intifada" sound to many of us like a call to not only kill the Jews in Israel, but to kill all the Jews worldwide.

As the rallies grew more raucous in the months that followed October 7 and the brutal military campaign in Gaza ground on, displays of what is indisputably antisemitism grew worse in certain quarters. In Oakland, a large public menorah was dismantled and pieces of it were thrown into Lake Merritt. About two weeks prior, an Oakland city council meeting held to debate a ceasefire resolution devolved into conspiracy. During the public comment period, one woman claimed that Israel had killed its own citizens on October 7. When one Jewish participant asked that the Oakland City Council amend the ceasefire resolution to include a condemnation of Hamas, someone in the audience said, "Heil Hitler." By early January 2024, at least thirty Jewish families residing in Oakland had applied to move their children to different school districts.

The following June, in Los Angeles, protesters blocked the entrance of an Orthodox synagogue, Adas Torah, yelling at, shoving, and kicking Jewish men in yarmulkes trying to get inside to pray. About two weeks earlier, the Brooklyn Museum's director, who is Jewish, had red paint smeared across the entry to her apartment building; a banner hung there accused her of being a "white-supremacist Zionist." For months, activists had been targeting the Brooklyn Museum—home to artwork by dozens of progressive artists examining topics such as race, oppression, and postcolonialism—and demanding that the museum disclose its list of donors and investments, and divest from any linked to Israel. Still, it's impossible to see the vandalism of a Jewish museum director's home—someone personally and professionally unconnected to Israel's current government—as anything but antisemitic. That same week, pro-Palestine protesters took over a New York City subway car, one of them leading chants of "Raise your hand if you're a Zionist" before adding, "This is your chance to get out." This was on a random subway car, among a random assortment of people. No one had any earthly idea what anyone else there thought about the state of Israel, or anything else under the sun for that matter. There is only one conclusion we can draw from a man demanding that "Zionists" identify themselves and leave the train. He meant Jews.

JEWS AND MANY others of goodwill would like to believe that signs, chants, and outbursts of wanton harassment against Jews are the work of an isolated few and don't represent a poison spreading in society. But we know all too well from our history that the careless use of antisemitic language and themes too often results in far more severe consequences. So I have tried on several occasions—in interviews I've given, speeches I've made, and in private conversations—to communicate the distress American Jews have been feeling about the growing antisemitism on the left. One of my greatest worries is that, because so many are so outraged by the terrible loss of life in Gaza, our message regarding this threat may fall on deaf ears.

This became apparent to me in a meeting I had in late 2023. On October 8, just hours after the deadliest terrorist attack against Jews on Israeli soil, the New York City chapter of the Democratic Socialists of America (DSA) promoted on social media a pro-Palestinian rally to be held in Times Square that afternoon. When I later saw the photos and videos from the rally, it almost looked like a demonstration in support of the terrorist attack. Several rallygoers appeared jubilant and were heard to be chanting the number of dead Israeli Jews, as if the October 7 attack were a heroic act. One attendee was even pictured displaying an image of a swastika on their phone. It really shook me.

You might not expect it, given my more establishment

reputation, but I knew a few of the people who were leaders in some of the more militant protests. As with many groups and individuals across the ideological spectrum with which I do not see eye to eye, I am willing to work with them on areas of mutual interest where a greater good can be accomplished. It is part of my role as representative of a big and diverse state like New York. I have often told them we have a symbiotic relationship: You push policies on the outside—on the streets—and on the instances when I agree with you, I'll seek a progressive outcome on the inside. These leaders and I had worked together successfully on local issues like opposing the construction of an environmentally unsafe natural gas plant and helping taxi drivers get paid by loan companies that were screwing them over. We had built up some trust and developed open lines of communication. Shortly after that October 8 demonstration, I received a letter from those leaders requesting a conversation about the situation in Gaza. The letter was perfectly respectful, earnest even; there was no name-calling. I was touched and hoped that we could find a way to understand one another, especially after the controversial rally in Times Square. I called them and told them that I wanted to sit down together to try to see each other's point of view.

The protest leaders drove down to Washington one weekday, and we spent maybe three or four hours talking. We began with the events that troubled all of us, the loss of so many innocent lives. I told them how much I deplored what had happened to so many children, both in Southern Israel on October 7 and in the Gaza Strip in the days and weeks since. I told them I was actively lobbying the Israeli government to do more to minimize civilian casualties in the Gaza Strip. I had hoped that they would see we valued the same things, that we both cherished human life, freedom, and dignity, and understood that a just peace was the only way to guarantee these for all people. They told me how angry they were at Israel and how they felt a moral obligation to stop Israel from killing any more civilians in Gaza. I said I understood where they were coming from, and I started to explain that based on our history, Jews, like everyone else, needed a homeland, and that Jews had a right to protect that homeland from terrorism. I told them that I thought some of the protests were going too far and might be provoking antisemitism. We were both deeply hurt by what was going on in the world.

But there was no resolution. I don't know if either of us was hoping for a change in outlook from the other, or some new path forward; maybe we both just wanted to be heard and understood. Unfortunately, I sensed that my concerns seemed insufficient to them compared to the suffering of the Palestinians. Maybe they believed that because I cared about Israelis as much as I do, I couldn't fully appreciate what they were saying. And so what began as an earnest attempt to bridge a divide ended on a note of quiet resignation. The distance between us was larger than we both realized, and we were both products of our distinct histories and viewpoints. I think we all left the meeting with the same feeling: not angry, but sad. To this day, I hope they came away with a better understanding of the deep roots of antisemitism and why Jews need a homeland of their own. I certainly came away with a better sense of their anguish as well. Shortly after our meeting, the same militant groups, including the two leaders I met with, resumed protesting in front of my apartment. They have continued on their path, and I have continued on mine.

Just as I believe Republicans need to speak out against antisemitism on the right, I believe it is imperative for Democrats to speak out against antisemitism on the left. For that reason, I was one of the very first Democratic members of Congress to do so. I gave a major address on the floor of the Senate condemning antisemitism on the left and enumerating its many guises. I hope many more Democrats will join me in that effort. I believe that those on the left who might be veering into antisemitism will pay far more attention to criticism from Democrats than from the right, which regularly attacks all condemnation of Israel.

As Jews throughout America and particularly on college campuses feel increasingly less safe, as Jewish community leaders become targets for far-left protests, as important liberal groups twist themselves in knots over issues related to Israel and antisemitism, I have struggled to come up with the right response. Unlike antisemitism on the far right, which is almost always deliberate, antisemitism on the left, while just as harmful, can sometimes be less intentional. What begins as protest or speech motivated by righteous anger can tip over into accusations that cast too wide a net of blame and use language that becomes a permission structure for, and often evolves into, antisemitism. It's also plausible, sometimes, that antisemitism may be voiced by individuals or groups who use it cynically to further their cause, gain supporters, or attract attention to their organization. What I've really struggled with—what I've always struggled with—is how to deal with those who are not inclined to listen to the other side because their righteousness is absolute. They are the ones most likely to go too far and by accident, carelessness, or design make antisemitism, not simply anti-Israel sentiment, acceptable to larger portions of the population.

Some of them may say, *So what?* So what if the criticism goes a little too far? Civilians are being killed in Gaza. Children are starving. If we say or do a few things that you may feel are a smidge antisemitic, it pales in comparison. After all, the Jews are strong. Israel is strong. They don't face any real danger, at least not like the acute danger that Palestinians face. And yes, even some Jews are out on the streets, too, distressed by what Israel is doing in the name of Jewish safety, protesting these very things, sometimes even shouting these very slogans.

But one action that is legitimate—strongly felt protest—should not excuse another that is not—blatant antisemitism. The danger to Jews from rising antisemitism is much more real and pressing than they would like to believe.

There have been two forms of antisemitism from the left, different in their own ways but each dangerous. One form is overt and can sometimes be the handiwork of lone actors. Boycotting or defacing Jewish-owned businesses. Blockading religious Jews from prayer in their houses of worship. Vandalizing the homes of Jewish leaders. Tearing down posters with photographs of the Israeli hostages being held in Gaza. These actions are mean-spirited, hurtful, and wrong, but we know how to handle them: We call them out and seek accountability and punishment for the perpetrators. The other form of antisemitism that Jews have witnessed from the left is less overt but equally dangerous: language or expressions that cross that blurry line between noisy protest and hate speech. There is a tendency by too many to write it off. *Well, they don't mean it. We know most of these protesters are not antisemitic. They're just kids saying stupid things. They're just getting carried away.*

But the reason Jews like me are so worried about rhetoric that starts to cross the line of antisemitism is that our history teaches us that there is an immense risk to Jews and to democratic societies when the door to antisemitism is pried open. Once the poison of antisemitism is injected into the bloodstream of society, it almost always circulates, especially in difficult times, and all too often leads to harm that goes far beyond words.

Our society needs a stiffer barrier between what we permit as legitimate protest and what we do not. Go after the Israeli government, I'd say, even if I disagree with you. Criticize the actions and policies of its military, as well as their devastating costs. But don't go over that edge. Don't think you can slur any Jew simply by calling them a Zionist. It is no less dangerous just because you use the word "Zionist" instead of "Jew," such as "close that Zionist deli" or "block that Zionist synagogue." Don't imply it's OK to kill Jews, in Israel or elsewhere, because you believe in the justice of an outcome "by any means necessary." Stop and wait and think hard before you accuse, without sufficient understanding, a country and a people of committing genocide—especially a people whose ancestors have been victims of genocide and who live in a country founded to prevent its repetition.

Now more than ever before in my lifetime, I fear the danger

of rising antisemitism. We live in troubled and turbulent times; people are looking for something and someone to blame. Extremism and bigotry on the American right are growing more powerful. Carrying the baggage of Jewish history on my back, I worry about antisemitism on the left in two ways. I worry first about those in the protest movement who are crossing the line and engaging in antisemitic rhetoric and actions. I worry also about the larger American left, which may look the other way and be too complacent or forgiving about those who exhibit antisemitism within their ranks. It's one of the many important reasons I decided to write this book: To warn my friends on the left. Be careful. Do not let passion overwhelm your better instincts. Do not let your desire for justice in the world lead you to bring a little more injustice into the world.

Hear us.

Be careful.

CHAPTER 8

AMERICAN JEWS AND ISRAEL

Israel. Eretz Yisrael. The land of milk and honey. The Holy Land. The Promised Land. Canaan. Palestine. There are many names for the small pocket of dust and desert wedged between Europe, Asia and Africa, and it means many different things to many different peoples. Within ethnic groups and religions— even among American Jews—people argue about its past, its present, and its future. To some of us, the more religious especially, Israel is a biblical homeland, a place of destiny that our people were promised by God. In the lyrics of the song from the film *Exodus*: "This land is mine / God gave this land to me." To others—the vast majority of us—Israel is a country of refuge, created in a time of moral emergency after the Holocaust to be the one state on Earth where Jews were guaranteed their safety because they oversaw it. With antisemitism on the rise, that imperative for Israel's existence has become even more strongly felt. Many American Jews, of all different backgrounds and affiliations, feel that we are a people as well as a religion and are entitled to a homeland like anyone else. Israel, therefore, is not a Jewish theocratic state, but a home for Jewish peoplehood and culture, and all that it entails. To other Jews still, many of them younger, Israel is merely a country, a piece of land buffeted by the forces of history and empire, created out of political necessity. To an extremely small but vocal minority of American Jews, there is no reason for a Jewish state at all.

Why Israel? Why do American Jews care so much about it?

I began this book with a theory: that knowledge of the Jewish-American experience, in all its diversity and dimension, is critical to understanding and fighting antisemitism in America. Recent events have convinced me that that alone is not enough. It's also necessary for people to think about how most Jewish-Americans understand Israel: Why we feel connected to it, why we care about it, why we defend it, and why we sometimes disagree with its actions. It is impossible to understand recent antisemitism in America without understanding the complex and multifaceted relationship Jewish-Americans have with Israel. And I think it's particularly important for younger Jews and non-Jews alike to understand Israel's history and the link between Jewish-Americans and Israel. In this chapter, I study the relationship between Jewish-Americans and Israel, and in the next, I explore the contemporary debates about Israel, its place in the world, and how some criticisms of Israel have led to antisemitism.

The links between Jews and Israel are complicated but, in most cases, strong and passionately felt. While the Jewish-American community is no monolith when it comes to Israel, and there are significant differences in views between the older and younger generations, and also among the denominations, the broad fact remains that more than 80 percent of American Jews consider caring about Israel an important or essential part of their Jewish identity. I count myself among that number. Why? I'm sure every Jewish person would give you a slightly different answer, but it hinges on some strange alchemy of heritage and history, as well as both Jewish and American pride. My personal connection to Israel is some combination of those factors, and I believe it is representative in many ways of how most Jewish-Americans feel.

GROWING UP, I heard a lot about Israel at the dinner table and at the synagogue but rarely in school or among my friends. I was born in 1950, shortly after the country was founded in 1948 and survived its first existential crisis, the War of Independence, when a group of surrounding Arab nations tried and failed to smother Israel in its infancy. Like the volunteers of the International Brigades during the Spanish Civil War, there were hundreds of passionate Jewish-Americans who went to join the fight. My friends and I would sometimes hang out in a playground between Ocean Parkway and Fifth Street in Brooklyn named after David "Mickey" Marcus, a U.S. Army colonel who had parachuted into Normandy on D-Day during the Second World War, commanded the Jerusalem Front during the 1948 War of Independence, and was tragically killed just six hours before the first ceasefire between the Arab states and Israel. Mickey Marcus from Brooklyn is remembered as the first general of the Israeli Defense Forces (IDF).

Even as a young child, I learned about the history of Israel. There was a special kind of pride in the role that America played in realizing the dream of a Jewish state. Until May 14, 1948, the land that is now Israel was under British control, a consequence of the Allied Powers' victory in World War I, which brought an end to four centuries of Ottoman Turkish rule in the region. During the Great War, in 1917, Britain made clear its intention to support "a national home for the Jewish people" in Palestine—enshrining that promise in what came to be known as the Balfour Declaration, which also called for safeguarding the religious and civil rights of the Palestinian Arab population, as well as the rights and political status of Jewish communities around the world. In 1947, with Britain's colonial mandate in Palestine set to expire the following year, the United Nations established a special committee to try to settle the question of the region's future governance. The committee proposed a partition: the creation of a Jewish state and an Arab state with international control over Jerusalem and surrounding areas of religious significance for Christians, Muslims, and Jews. President Truman was confronted with a difficult decision. More than six hundred thousand Jews were living in the area by then, but overall they were still a minority.

Would the United States support the UN partition plan? Would America back this novel idea of a small and fragile Jewish state against the diplomatically and economically powerful Arab states, which had oil, a commodity increasingly needed by the West? It was fiercely debated within the Truman administration. Some within the State Department harbored antisemitic attitudes, and many throughout the government whispered concerns to the White House that, given the onset of the Cold War, the Soviets could gain influence over the production and distribution of Middle Eastern oil if the United States aligned itself with the Jews. Truman's secretary of state, George Marshall—five-star general, hero of the Second World War, author of the Marshall Plan—argued against Israeli statehood for geopolitical strategic reasons. He feared an all-out war in the region, which could draw in the US military. The American oil companies were strongly opposed as well. Powerful voices were aligned against the nascent state of Israel. But there were voices on the other side too, much less powerful but righteous. Truman had a longtime army buddy named Eddie Jacobson, a Jewish-American with whom he went into business after the First World War. For a few years, the two had run a haberdashery, a common Jewish trade. During a critical time in the debate over Israel in 1948, Jacobson pleaded with the president to meet Chaim Weizmann, the former head of the World Zionist Organization. The man from Independence—the name of Truman's hometown in Missouri—became the first world leader to recognize Israel's independence, only eleven minutes after its creation. Immediately following Israel's declaration of independence, five Arab armies invaded. Compared to the newly constituted Israeli forces, less than two-thirds of whom were armed, the Arab armies had modern artillery and armored vehicles, a much larger population from which to draw, and better strategic positions on the battlefield. Nonetheless, after nine months of intense fighting, Israel prevailed.

Imagine how it must have felt to Jewish-Americans at the time, still reeling from the incomprehensible images of emaciated and defeated Jews being marched to the death camps, to see this new Jewish nation stand on its own two feet and defeat invading armies. How it must have felt to have their adopted homeland, America, place its awesome might behind the notion of Jewish self-determination while most of the world, for mercenary reasons (oil) or self-interest, was noncommittal or ready to abandon the idea, even after the devastation of the Holocaust. Though I was still very young at the time, it was impossible to miss the sense of community pride that Jewish-Americans felt about America's support for Israel's creation. It was instilled in me too.

For much of my early childhood in the 1950s, Israel remained a fledgling country. The seeds of development were being sown, but it was not yet a military, economic, or political power by any stretch of the imagination. While I didn't think about Israel on a daily basis—this incredibly foreign land of beaches and deserts and palm trees, of dates and almonds and spices—nonetheless, whenever I did, it inspired a powerful sense of pride. Somewhere, people like me were laboring to build a nation of their own.

At Hebrew school, studying for our Bar Mitzvahs, we'd learn the history of the Jewish people in ancient Canaan and recount the stories of the Old Testament. These were names and places that we could now find on a map of this new Jewish state of Israel. It seemed, perhaps, like we had always belonged there. We also might learn a fact or two about the modern state. What were the names of the big cities? Only three were of note: Jerusalem, Tel Aviv, and Haifa. The nation was about the population of Kansas and, in terms of size, roughly equivalent to New Jersey.

By the time I had become a teenager, even though I was halfway across the world from Israel, I remember feeling a deep connection to it, as both an American and as a Jew. The 1960s were a time of growing tensions in the region. Stung from their defeat in the Israeli War of Independence, as well as Israel's role in the 1956 Suez Crisis, the Arab nations tried to isolate and strangle the new country in other ways, through organizing boycotts of Israeli goods and travelers as well as blacklisting international companies that traded with or had a presence in Israel. When several of the world's airlines boycotted Israel so that they could keep flying to Arab destinations, I rooted for Air France because it was among the airlines that continued to fly to Tel Aviv. I even preferred Coca-Cola to Pepsi because they did business in Israel even though it led to Coke being boycotted by Arab countries.

In 1967, Egypt built up its military forces on Israel's border and began a blockade of the Straits of Tiran, an important shipping lane between the Red Sea and southern Israel; these actions helped lead to the Six-Day War. Again, multiple Arab armies (Egypt, Jordan, and Syria, with support also from Lebanon, Iraq, and Saudi Arabia) joined forces against Israel, fighting on its own. I remember walking alone, in silence, to class at James Madison High School with a transistor radio held to my ear, listening to the news reports in June 1967, praying to God that Israel would survive. Once again, plucky little Israel proved much stronger than most of the world expected. It wiped out the Egyptian air force in a preemptive strike, which gave Israel's air force, only nineteen years young, supremacy over the skies. Israel captured the Sinai Peninsula, later returned to Egypt as part of the Camp David Accords, which normalized relations between the two countries in 1979.

Just two decades earlier, Jewish-Americans were deeply

scarred by the impression that the Jews of Europe had gone meekly to their fate during the Holocaust. While there were many instances of Jewish rebellions and daring escapes, there was also a feeling in America of shame. It might not have been fair or rational, but many had thought, *How could the Jews let the Nazis do this to us? Why did so many let themselves be marched into the camps with little or no resistance?* Israel was born in the shadow of that trauma and that perceived shame. Over the first few decades of Israel's existence, during the War of Independence and especially the Six-Day War, its successful military instilled in Jews everywhere a renewed sense of pride in the Jewish ability to fight back. It cannot be underestimated how important this feeling was to Jewish-Americans at the time.

Throughout my youth, for me and most Jewish-Americans, the shadow of the Holocaust was always hanging over us. On every street where Jewish families lived, there were a few who had been lucky enough to survive the Shoah (Hebrew for "calamity") or else had close friends or relatives who had. It was not uncommon to have a neighbor or two who would roll up their sleeves to show my friends and me the identification numbers tattooed on their arms—the unmistakable mark of the concentration camps and a visual reminder of how the Nazis considered the Jews less than human, a mere number. These older men and women wanted to make sure the younger generation knew what had happened.

As a teenager, I dated a girl whose parents were ice-skating champions in Poland before each was sent to a separate concentration camp. Miraculously, both survived, reunited after the war, and got married. When I asked her how her mother had made it through the camp, she wouldn't answer me, refusing to bring to mind the unspeakable horrors her mother must have endured at the hands of the Nazi soldiers. In every Jewish house, discussions at the dinner table would often turn to the Holocaust, and to questions that Jews could never answer: *How could something so horrible have happened? How did the world allow something like this to happen? Why wasn't God there to prevent it?* All of this strengthened our belief that the world needed a place where Jews could go if another Nazi regime ever came to power. It strengthened our resolve to support Israel.

I first visited Israel myself when I was twenty-one years old, for my brother's Bar Mitzvah in 1971. My brother is the youngest of my siblings, and my father had decided that the last Bar Mitzvah in the family was going to be in the Holy Land itself. The history of our people was there and many of the great Jewish sages, he reasoned, had come from the area. Having your Bar Mitzvah at the Western Wall remains a popular tradition for Jews from all over the world. This was now more than fifty years ago, but I remember seeing Jerusalem for the first time like it was yesterday. We were driving from the airport in Tel Aviv on the old highway to Jerusalem, which, before bending into the valley of the city, offered an expansive view of that ancient skyline: sand-colored stone roofs nestled around the great synagogues, the spires of churches, the golden dome of the Temple Mount rising above the old walls of David's kingdom. It was an almost magical sight. My hair stood on edge. I sensed, instinctively, why it was the holy city for three great religions.

Another thing struck me when I visited Israel: Jews held every occupation. There were not only Jewish doctors and teachers, but Jewish janitors and Jewish garbagemen. Imagine a Jewish garbageman! I had never seen one before. Oddly, it made me proud. Here, Jews could be everything.

Only a few years later, once again, the Jewish-American community worried that Israel would be driven into the sea. There was another Arab invasion of Israel on Yom Kippur in 1973, launched as a surprise attack on the holiest Jewish holiday of the year. Once again Israel would prevail, but the Arab nations, in reaction to Israel's victory, imposed an oil embargo against any country that was supporting Israel, including the United States. It precipitated a global oil crisis. American Jews were deeply afraid that the skyrocketing price of oil could lead to inflation and would turn the United States against Israel for the first time. In a few American cities, you would see the odd bumper sticker or two that said BURN JEWS, NOT OIL, but these would, fortunately, turn out to be extremely dissonant voices, and the United States stuck with Israel. The memory of the Holocaust and why Israel existed still loomed large in the American mind. *What a great country America is*, we thought again, *how good it has been to the Jews!*

It's hard today to imagine Israel—now the dominant military power in the region, backed by the dominant military power in the world, the United States—as a country that could, at any moment, be destroyed by its neighbors. But that was how it felt to most American Jews, and certainly to Israeli Jews. Israel was a nation of 3 million surrounded by Arab nations, well-armed and with 50 million people, hellbent, it seemed to us, on its destruction. The Israeli journalist Ari Shavit described the feeling in his book *My Promised Land*: "Our cities seemed to be built on shifting sand. Our houses never seemed quite stable. Even as my nation grew stronger and wealthier, I felt it was profoundly vulnerable. I realized how exposed we are, how constantly intimidated.... There is always the fear that one day daily life will freeze like Pompeii's."

Today, younger Americans have grown up knowing only an Israel that is strong and prosperous. It has created the impression that it has always been so and will always be so—that threats to Jewish life in Israel are not so grave. But to most older Jewish-Americans and many younger ones—and for Israeli Jews, for whom suicide bombs and knife attacks, rocket fire and emergency siren alerts have long been part of everyday life— Israel will always feel like a nation in the shadow of a great volcano. It's the reason October 7 hit a deep and sensitive nerve for American Jews. For those of us who have grown up knowing Israel as being under constant existential threat, it recalled our fears, built up over Israel's founding decades, of the possibility of its annihilation. Despite knowing that Israel today has an extremely capable and resourceful military, we warily watch Iran—a nation dedicated to Israel's destruction and on the verge of building a nuclear weapon—send wave after wave of missiles at this strip of a country, and we remember the days when Israel seemed so small and alone.

Discussions in the United States about its "special relationship" with Israel, I believe, would be more constructive if people understood better why most Jewish-Americans developed a protective feeling toward Israel, and why that feeling persists even if Israel has managed to successfully defend itself against groups trying to destroy it. It would increase understanding of those who participate in a protest or debate about Israel if they studied its history, with a mind open to the deeply rooted emotional connection that so many Jewish people around the world feel for a sliver of land that is a place of heritage and pride.

As I GOT older, my feelings toward Israel grew more nuanced, molded and perhaps sharpened by its critics and opponents. When I was a student at Harvard, I began to meet students with radical politics who considered Israel an offshoot of America's global imperialism, an emblem of its overreach and militarism. I remember the day in November 1970 when Jewish students invited the Israeli foreign minister, Abba Eban, to give a lecture on campus to combat the growing anti-Israel sentiment among some of the leftist students. More than two thousand people gathered in Sanders Theatre, one of Harvard's largest auditoriums, to listen to Ambassador Eban. The members of SDS sat in the gallery and hung a banner: FIGHT ZIONIST IMPERIALISM. When Eban began to speak, they tried to shout him down. Eban pointed his finger up at the protesters in the gallery.

He calmly, but forcefully, in his Etonian tones—he was raised in Britain but made aliya to Israel—delivered a statement I will never forget. "I am talking to you up there in the gallery," I remember him saying.

Every time a people get their statehood, you applaud it. The Nigerians, the Pakistanis, the Zambians, you applaud. There's only one people, when they gain statehood, who you don't applaud, you condemn it—and that is the Jewish people. We Jews are used to that. We have lived with a double standard through the centuries. There were always things the Jews couldn't do. Everyone could be a farmer, but not the Jew. Everyone could be a carpenter, but not the Jew. Everyone could move to Moscow, but not the Jew. And everyone can have their own state, but not the Jew. There is a word for that—antisemitism—and I accuse you in the gallery of it.

Eban's words were so powerful, the protesters slinked away. They did not attack Israel for my remaining years at Harvard.

I cheered. He had expressed a deeper truth about Israel's critics that not only won the argument that day but strengthened my own resolve to defend Israel's right to exist. That feeling of deep unfairness—that Israel and Jews were held alone and apart from all other nations and peoples clamoring for self-determination—resonated with so many Jewish-Americans. We understood Israel to be a part of those movements, a consequence of the breakup of great European empires and territorial mandates in the Middle East, with all of the messiness and displacement that entails. It was a modern, *post*-colonial state, for a people that had never had one before. The opposition on campus revealed to me that Israel's right to exist was not only being challenged in the Middle East and at the UN but in certain corners of American politics. I realized I felt a need to defend it.

My involvement with the Harvard Young Democrats opened my eyes to a different type of opposition Israel faced—institutional and political opposition. There was one new senator who came to my attention: Mark Hatfield from Oregon. He'd been elected in 1966 and would retain his seat for the next thirty years. Senator Hatfield was a former governor, a prominent Baptist layman, and a Rockefeller Republican, liberal on most issues of the day, but fervently anti-Israel. (Later, during the 1980s and '90s when he was the chairman of the Senate Committee on Appropriations, he always opposed legislation that was friendly to Israel, whether it was economic aid, military assistance, or merely symbolic.) One of the things that bothered me about this senator was that he would come to New York to raise money from the Jewish community. There were many Jewish liberals who were antiwar and who wanted to support Rockefeller Republican–type candidates but had no idea of Senator Hatfield's anti-Israel positions. It just got under my skin, not only because he never told the Jewish community about his views on Israel, but because the Jewish community was so unaware and even gullible that they were eagerly helping someone who was working against one of their most important priorities. So in 1970, as a college junior, I wrote to the major Jewish organizations in New York and got hold of their contribution lists. I raised $3,000 from leaders of the community, then used that money to send a letter to all of Senator Hatfield's Jewish contributors in New York detailing whatever I could glean of his positions on Israel from the papers.

It was a harbinger of things to come. After I entered Congress, I took on issues that concerned Jewish refugees and Israel, joining a movement in American politics to support Soviet Jews who wished to emigrate but required an exit visa from the Kremlin to be able to do so. They had suffered years of brutal repression, intimidation, and violence at the hands of the Stalinist regime, so we campaigned to allow more Russian Jews to immigrate to America. By the late '80s, we had succeeded in pushing the George H. W. Bush administration to raise the ceiling for Soviet refugee admissions. Tens of thousands arrived, and I helped many of them settle in Brighton Beach, where Soviet Jewish refugees from an earlier wave had also settled.

At the time, it was a neighborhood with many vacant, four-story walk-up apartments right next to the ocean. Hoping that it would remind them of Odessa, we helped steer them there. During the same period, because the American immigration process was politicized and funding for refugee resettlement was tight—and also because Israel was keen to have more Jews make *aliya*—hundreds of thousands of Soviet Jews moved to Israel, serving yet again as a reminder that a Jewish homeland was needed in the world. Unlike in the 1940s, there was now an Israel that would gladly accept and give shelter to Jews persecuted around the world. Today, Russian-speaking Jews alone account for more than 15 percent of Israel's population.

I felt that it was part of my duty to defend Israel's right to exist, and to support, however I could, the friendship between our two countries. For most of my political career, those were not terribly controversial viewpoints. Once Israel firmly established itself as a regional power by the late 1970s, the tumult of its first few decades settled down. So did most of the political opposition in the United States. Israel was a stalwart ally, a democratic partner for our country in a region of despotic and theocratic regimes. But even in this period of relative strength, security, and support, the fact that Israeli citizens were routinely subject to terrorism, including the massacre of Israeli athletes at the 1972 Munich Olympics and the hijacking of a passenger flight from Tel Aviv in 1976, reminded American Jews of the constant threat that Israel and Israelis faced around the world.

As a legislator, my priority was never to support a particular Israeli prime minister or party, but rather to do what I could as a part of America's political system to keep Israel and its interests secure. Practically speaking, it's not so different from how many other senators and representatives take an interest in various foreign policy issues. My other priority was to keep American support for Israel a matter of bipartisan concern. It was the only way to ensure that it would endure. If support for Israel became something that only one party valued, it would ebb and flow with elections; and because most legislation requires bipartisan support to succeed, it would make it harder to do anything for Israel. So whenever I carried legislation related to Israel, I always tried to find a Republican cosponsor to work with me. The Israel-America relationship, I believed, was supposed to be above politics.

For much of Israel's existence, the rhetoric of its politicians and the policies of its governments did little to undercut American support. Prime ministers and Israeli policies would change, but American support would remain staunch. But Prime Minister Benjamin "Bibi" Netanyahu's most recent years in power, and in particular his coalition government with the Israeli far right and the impression that he favored one American political party over the other, have changed the status quo and pushed a good number of Jewish-Americans away from Israel's government. It's important to understand how we got to this point.

I HAVE KNOWN Bibi personally for decades, and our relationship has evolved significantly over time. His older brother Yonatan "Yoni" Netanyahu, the hero of Entebbe and the only Israeli soldier who was killed during that daring rescue mission of Israeli hostages from Uganda, had been my freshman-year classmate at Harvard. He transferred to Jerusalem's Hebrew University in 1968. While I didn't know Yoni personally, the fact that we had been on campus together helped foster a relationship with Bibi. By the time we met in the 1980s, Bibi was working his way up the ladder of Israeli politics via the diplomacy route. Back then, I admired his intelligence and his committed defense of the state of Israel. We became friends.

In the mid-1980s, when Bibi was the Israeli ambassador to the United Nations, he was visiting New York with a delegation of Israeli economists. In between events at the UN building in Midtown Manhattan, I invited the lot of them over for dinner at my apartment in Brooklyn with my wife, Iris. At one point in the evening, over pastrami sandwiches, the conversation turned toward Israel's economy. After an initial burst of development in the early years, it had stagnated. The spike in oil prices and an increase in defense expenditure had led to high rates of inflation and growing budget deficits. Recently the government had introduced a stabilization plan, which relied on currency devaluation and price controls. Bibi was asked: What was going to happen to the economy over the next few years? There was a two-liter bottle of Diet Pepsi on the white linen runner. Bibi reached for it, unscrewed the cap, jabbed his thumb into the bottle, and began to shake.

"You want to know what's going to happen to Israel's economy?" he said. "You can't see anything happening now, but watch."

He took his thumb out. The soda sprayed all over the ceiling, the food, the guests. Everyone was shocked but we all laughed. Not too long after, the Israeli economy indeed rebounded and enjoyed many years of significant growth. The future prime minister of Israel was apologetic, promising, in jest, to cover the cost of cleaning our kitchen and dining room.

We stayed on relatively good terms for many years after that, during his first stint as prime minister between 1996 and 1999, as finance minister in 2003–2005, and again through much of his second decade-long stint as prime minister (2009–2021), which began during the Obama administration and lasted through Trump's presidency and beyond. His term as finance minister was a notable success. Many of the reforms passed during his tenure helped turn Israel from an emerging market into a global economic force, leading the world in many areas of technology. I certainly appreciated his stalwart defense of Israel's security as prime minister as well. By the time Netanyahu's second stint as prime minister rolled around, multiple Israeli proposals for a two-state solution had been rejected by the Palestinians. A focus on economic growth and military security was both politically popular and necessary.

Around the same time, however, I saw the first hints that Bibi was willing to depart from the tradition of keeping Israel's relations in America above the partisan fray. While President Obama was seeking a nuclear agreement with Iran, Prime Minister Netanyahu was invited to address Congress by the Republican leader of the House, John Boehner, without the approval or permission of the president, an unprecedented situation. Netanyahu's acceptance of the invitation was an indication that he was no longer feeling constrained by the need to keep the relationship between the United States and Israel completely bipartisan and within the norms of accepted diplomacy.

On the substance, however, I agreed with Bibi about the Iran nuclear deal. I believed that the agreement should have required Iran to stop arming Hamas, Hezbollah, and other proxies that were a threat to Israel. I was one of the few Democrats who opposed the deal negotiated by President Obama. The October 7 attacks by Hamas and more recent rocket fire in northern Israel by Hezbollah have reinforced my view that it was the correct rationale. Bibi was grateful not only because I agreed with him, but that I opposed the president of my own party in voting against the deal.

My relationship with Bibi, however, took a serious turn once Donald Trump became president. Internationally, Netanyahu started playing favorites with far-right political parties in other countries, cozying up to illiberal regimes such as Hungary's, provided they expressed support for Israel. Alongside Ron Dermer, an American-born former Republican Party operative, whom Netanyahu appointed as Israel's ambassador to the United States, Netanyahu unreservedly embraced the first Trump administration and made overtures to align Israel with this new breed of ultra-right-wing Republicans in the United States. My concern wasn't that Bibi was aligning himself with Republicans who supported Israel; I was concerned that his actions might ruin relationships with Democrats who supported Israel.

It came to a head in 2019 when I met with Netanyahu in Washington, D.C. where he was scheduled to speak at AIPAC's annual conference and also to meet President Trump. Bibi came to see me at the Capitol and brought Ron Dermer with him. I invited the prime minister in but asked Dermer to wait outside.

I wanted to confront Bibi, directly and alone, to try to salvage the long history of bipartisan support for Israel in America, in my mind one of Israel's greatest assets.

I said to Bibi, "I understand Israel's priorities and I care about Israel's safety, as you do. And I agree with you that the greatest short-term threat to Israel are the rockets that Iran gives to Hamas and Hezbollah, which could kill thousands of Israelis. But the greatest medium- and long-term threat to Israel is if America loses faith in Israel. By embracing Trump and associating yourself with only one political party in America, the Republicans, you are going to lose half of America, including the left and many young people." I told him, "You have got to change for the sake of Israel. You have to show America that you're not picking sides." I counseled him to make Israel's case not just to conservatives and on conservative media. "You can't just go on Sean Hannity," I said, "you have to make the case for supporting Israel on Rachel Maddow too."

He promised he'd do it, but he never did. Egged on by members of his party at home, Netanyahu's embrace of both the hard right in Israel and the Trump administration only grew tighter, and his actions alienated Democrats even more. Taking a cue from Bibi's embrace of Trump, some of the more right-wing partisan Republicans in America have tried to turn Israel into a wedge issue. Instead of attacking individual Democrats with whom they disagreed about Israel, which is legitimate, certain Republicans endeavored to label the entire Democratic Party as anti-Israel, which is false: The vast majority of Democrats in the House and Senate strongly support Israel. This damaged the concept that support for Israel should always be bipartisan and diminished support for Israel as a whole.

The past few years of Prime Minister Netanyahu's government, both before and after October 7, have seen a continuation of many of these trends. Domestically, Netanyahu seemed to lose regard for moderation and consensus, moving his government further to the right while appointing ministers to his cabinet who were bigoted and even Jewish supremacists. Finance Minister Bezalel Smotrich and National Security Minister Itamar Ben-Gvir have voiced abominable views and pursued extremist policies. They have needlessly antagonized the Muslim Palestinians living in Jerusalem by disrespecting their holiest sites (the Dome of the Rock), distributed assault rifles to far-right settlers in the West Bank, called for Israel's annexation of the West Bank, and the building of Jewish settlements in the middle of Gaza to propel a "voluntary emigration" of Palestinians living in these lands. They have expressed the desire to create "a Jewish State from the river to the sea," and Smotrich went so far as to suggest that the starvation of Gazans was justified and moral. To most Americans, their casual disregard for Palestinian lives and dignity is repulsive.

Netanyahu's coalition has grown only more hawkish since Hamas attacked Israel on October 7. The ensuing and awful loss of innocent life in Gaza has left many feeling that Israel has not done enough to minimize casualties or provide adequate food, water, and medicine to civilians, in part to appease the right-wingers in Netanyahu's government. In my view, this is the number-one reason Israel is losing support in America. Also confounding is the unwillingness on the part of the Netanyahu government to seriously entertain proposals that could lead to a two-state solution—the only path to an enduring peace between Israelis and Palestinians. The United States has been engaged in diplomatic discussions with Saudi Arabia as a possible broker and regional guarantor of a two-state solution. The Saudis have appeared willing to provide both funds to help rebuild Gaza and political, moral, and financial support to create a moderate Palestinian leadership in the West Bank and Gaza Strip. The Saudis, in return, ask for the Israeli government to support a moderate, demilitarized Palestinian state several years in the future that would live alongside the Jewish state, creating for the first time in decades a realizable scenario for peace in the Middle East. Once Israel would announce such support, moderate Arab Sunni states would join the Saudis in this effort.

The contours of such an agreement would likely be acceptable to most of the Israeli people, its army, and its leaders. But Bibi himself, needing the support of extremists like Smotrich and Ben-Gvir to maintain his government, has thus far not been open to it. He does not seem willing to call for a two-state solution, foreclosing the possibility of a real political settlement after so much bloodshed, even after the dramatic weakening of Hamas and Hezbollah by Israeli forces, which has made such an agreement possible. All of this has deepened the divide between many American Jews and Netanyahu and caused the traditional support for Israel in America to erode.

According to the most recent Pew survey, nine in ten U.S. Jews have a favorable view of the Israeli people. Nine in ten find the way Hamas attacked Israel on October 7 to be unacceptable; nine in ten say Israel's reasons for fighting Hamas are justified. Only six in ten say the way Israel is carrying out its response to the Hamas attack is acceptable. And only half of America's Jews hold a favorable view of the current Israeli government—and the percentage among all Americans is even lower.

I BELIEVE I speak for most Jewish-Americans when I say that we support, first and foremost, Israel's right to exist. We want to see an Israel that is safe and prosperous, and that certainly colors the way we see groups like Hamas, which will fight to the hilt to see that there is no Israel. We feel, in a deeply personal way, the unfairness of the double standard when the world treats Israel differently than any other nation. And for many decades, the majority of American Jews, myself among them, have wanted to see the creation of a viable, demilitarized Palestinian state, one that could live in peace and dignity side by side with Israel. That was also the policy of the Israeli government for many years, and today it remains the policy of the U.S. government. Today, as in the past, more American Jews favor a two-state solution than any other outcome in the region, admittedly in greater percentages than Israeli Jews, who bear the scars of decades of failed peace processes, including moments when they saw Palestinian leadership, often at the last minute, pull out of a potential agreement.

While there is much consensus, feelings within the Jewish-American community have recently become more divided and more conflicted. The pride many feel about America's support for the only liberal democracy in the Middle East deflates when that democracy becomes less liberal and less democratic. Many Jewish-Americans I know who are strong supporters of Israel are principled critics of the current Netanyahu regime. Some younger Jewish-Americans participate in protests for Palestinian rights and statehood, and they deplore, as do most Jewish-Americans, the high number of civilian casualties in Gaza. Some of them feel alienated from Israel and don't want the American government to unconditionally support its government.

I have not hesitated to criticize Netanyahu's views, statements, and policies that I feel make Israel less democratic and less safe. As the highest-ranking elected Jewish official in American history, I felt an obligation as someone who cherishes Israel to show Jews and non-Jews alike—in America, in Israel, and around the world—that you could disagree with Netanyahu and his government and still love Israel; that you could challenge some of Israel's politicians and policies, particularly those that have resulted in a high death toll in Gaza, and still believe it deserves strong and steady military and economic support. Over the course of my career, and since October 7 especially, I have backed every proposal to provide Israel with the security assistance it needs to keep its people safe. Like many Jewish-Americans, I am glad that Israel has recently eliminated the leaders of both Hamas and Hezbollah, two terrorist groups who not only threaten and murder Israelis but impoverish and terrorize populations in Gaza, Lebanon, and beyond. While the suffering in Gaza is heartbreaking, we're mindful that a good portion of the blame falls on Hamas for using the civilian population as human shields. It's possible to be proud of Israel's operational successes against these terrorist networks and the security that Israel has gained because of it, and also critical of some aspects of its military campaign in Gaza. Despite the differences Jewish-Americans might have with Israel's current government, nearly all of us want to see that a strong, safe, and secure Israel continues to exist in the world.

One of my greatest fears is that Israel will become a pariah state, abandoned by both America and the world, disenchanting particularly the younger generations. I gave a speech last March from the Senate floor stating the view that you could disagree with Netanyahu and still strongly support Israel. The speech intended to arrest the further isolation of Israel from the American public and give solace to those who were struggling to reconcile their love for Israel with their disagreement with Netanyahu's policies. I remain fiercely proud that I gave that speech.

WHILE MY GRANDFATHER immigrated to America and found opportunity, many of his siblings, cousins, aunts and uncles, and other family members remained in Eastern Europe. When I was a young boy, it was explained to me why many branches of our family tree had stopped growing forever—in fact, all the branches other than my grandfather's and his three siblings who came to America.

In the summer of 1941, the Nazis invaded the Soviet Union and began their eastward push toward Moscow. When the Nazis reached Galicia, most of which is now in western Ukraine, they encountered in Chortkiv one of the oldest Jewish communities in the area. Local records show that the Jews of Chortkiv had been there at least since 1616 (the date engraved on the oldest preserved tombstone found in the old Jewish cemetery). The Schumer family was among those Jews.

My grandmother and then my father would tell me what

must have been an abridged version of what happened to my family in Chortkiv (many of the details were either unknown or unsuitable for a child). Our family used to be of some prominence, they'd say, because they were large in number and lived right on the town square. So when the Nazis came across my great-grandmother's family house, they asked her—the matriarch of the family and the widow of the locally revered rabbi—to gather her children, her grandchildren, and her great-grandchildren on the porch of her home. As more than thirty people emerged from that house on the town square, aged three months to eighty-five years old, the Nazis forced the Jewish residents of the town to gather around and watch. The Nazis were going to make an example of this big family. It was to be a demonstration of one of two things: the merits of compliance or the consequences of resistance.

The Nazis issued a simple ultimatum to my great-grandmother, Frima.

"You are coming with us," they said.

She refused.

In front of the Jews of the town, they machine-gunned every last one of them. The babies, the elderly, and everybody in between.

It is the custom of Ashkenazi Jews to honor the dead by naming newborn children after a lost ancestor. My sister Fran is named for our great-grandmother. These terrifying chapters in Jewish history are still with us, even in our names.

Most, if not all, Jewish-Americans carry with them stories similar to those of my great-grandmother. Most, if not all of us, heard these stories at a young age. They are imprinted on our hearts for as long as we live, filling us with an unspoken and ill-defined grief, a sense of having lost something vast and beautiful. At Yad Vashem, the Holocaust museum in Jerusalem, there is a space called the Children's Memorial. It is a simple box-shaped concrete structure, room for only a small group to huddle. Inside, it is completely dark, save the light from five candles. Mirrors, however, are placed all around at just the right angles to reflect the light in an infinite number of directions. It is meant to symbolize the idea that for every life lost in the Holocaust, there were an infinite number of lives lost, children that would never grow up, untold generations that would never be born. Six million Jews, 1.5 million of them children, were murdered in the Holocaust. The Children's Memorial reminds us that we cannot ever truly measure the number. Every few seconds, you hear the name, the age, the birthplace of a murdered child. On my last visit, I saw the picture of a six-year-old from Romania who looked uncannily like my daughter.

Sometimes as a kid, I tried to picture them, those long-distant Schumers, living half a world away and half a lifetime ago. Did they look like me? What kind of food did they eat? Did they ride their bikes on the weekend like I did? Who were their friends, neighbors, school crushes? Did they like to dance? If so, to what music? I never got very far in my imagination. I had too few details. To me, their lives were like the black-and-white photos in the family album, faded and inanimate.

What if they had survived? Would I have gone to visit them on summer holidays, swam in the placid river that runs through the town, hiked the forests around the village, greening with herbs? Would I have sat on that porch, kicking my feet on the floorboards, playing with my European cousins? Then I think:

What if there had been a country where they could have fled to, not so far and so alien as America, when they sensed trouble was brewing and war was coming? A place that all Jews knew would be a safe homeland. Would they have left then?

As an adult, I remember hearing how my grandfather reacted when he first saw Israel. It was the first time he had ever flown in a plane, and when he landed, stepping out of Ben Gurion Airport in Tel Aviv, he became overwhelmed by emotion and broke down in tears. It was deeply human—a moment of catharsis for a man whose family was uprooted and exterminated, finally setting foot in a place of refuge for his people. I know what crossed his mind because I've thought it too. How many of my aunts, uncles, cousins, nieces, and nephews would be alive today had Israel existed before World War II?

For many, that is how we see and understand Israel and its security. It is a land of last resort, a place you can go where you can be safe and be Jewish, even if all the nations of the world turn against us. Yad Vashem, like the old highway leading to Jerusalem, is built on a hilltop near the old city. As you walk out of the museum, the doors open onto a balcony overlooking Jerusalem, a reminder of what Jews were able to build out of the ashes of our greatest tragedy, that hope was possible beyond despair.

That sense—that conception of Israel—is what made the attack on October 7 so visceral for Jews. What if modern Israel, after all, isn't safe? What if this last sanctuary, too, were destroyed? Ultimately, the sum of the fears and the hopes of the Jewish people are intertwined with the fate of Israel, creating a link that is difficult to describe but nearly impossible to sever. Out of the darkness of century upon century of oppression, there was now this new light, a real place where Jewish freedom, ingenuity, and pride could flourish.

That contrast—the hope and security Israel promises to the Jewish people compared to the suffering of our forebears—gives it profound meaning. My great-grandmother in Chortkiv, for example, could scarcely have imagined that one day soon there would be a country for Jews. We had been scattered to the winds, foreigners in our own country, derided by our neighbors, forbidden to be farmers or tradesmen or academics, treated as scapegoats and second-class citizens. The idea that there would be a Jewish state, with Jewish politicians and Jewish policemen, Jewish grocers and Jewish garbagemen, where the street names would sound like our last names and our religious holidays would be national holidays—the idea would probably have sounded too strange to her.

Imagine telling the Jews of the ghettos that someday there would be a country called Israel. I think they would give a hearty guffaw and go on selling their wares. Imagine, instead, telling the Jews of Russia or Poland or Romania, chased from town to town by galloping hooves and burning torches, that there would one day be an entire country for people like them. Imagine, for a moment, if you could whisper to the young Jewish father, whom they came for one day and loaded onto a train, who was separated from his family, who was made to labor day after day and watch those wreaths of smoke rising under a silent blue sky. Imagine if you could tell him, one night, alone in the dark, that someday soon there would be a place where Jews like him could live in freedom and raise their families in peace.

If you could only tell him.

It is impossible to separate the idea of the state of Israel from the history of persecution and degradation of the Jewish people. There is a special and almost indescribable pride that comes from knowing, despite all the horrors, that after two millennia of wandering the desert, the Jewish people would finally return home.

WHEN I FIRST started learning the details of the October 7 massacre, I was in China with a bipartisan delegation of my fellow senators to meet President Xi Jinping. We had just concluded a discussion about opening Chinese markets to American companies, and the Israeli ambassador to China was summoned to give us a briefing. The horrors were just coming into focus. The Israeli ambassador shared with me the story of what happened in one of the kibbutzim, called Be'eri. Hamas terrorists had entered the kibbutz in the early hours of October 7 and killed more than one hundred Jewish residents: the babies, the elderly, and everyone in between.

I thought of my ancestors on the porch in Galicia.

CHAPTER 9

ANTISEMITISM AND ISRAEL

A day after the October 7 attacks, instead of staying with our congressional delegation in China after meeting with President Xi, I decided that I needed to go to Israel. During times of crisis and fear, Israelis and Jews around the world tend to feel alone, a legacy of a deep historical sense of abandonment. I felt that I had to be there to demonstrate America's solidarity with the country. I wanted to tell the Israeli people that America had their back.

In the course of my visit, I sat with the families of some of the Israelis who were killed in the assault. I've sat with them many times since, as well as with some of the family members of those who were taken hostage. I cannot imagine what they went and are still going through. Every hour must carry enough anguish and grief to fill a lifetime. I encouraged the families to tell me about their loved ones; what they were like; about the things and people they loved and lived for. I encouraged the parents of the hostages to tell me about their hopes for their children's future when they returned. If they returned. All one can do is to try to be there for them and provide some sense of comfort, maybe even a degree of hope. More often than not, we did little but sit and shed tears together. Now, well over a year since they were captured, nearly sixty-five hostages, including four Americans, remain in captivity, as do the bodies of thirty-five others.

During those early meetings, I was at least able to express to the families that I would stand up for Israel's right to defend itself. I told them America would push as hard as it could for the safe return of the hostages. In those moments, I felt like I was doing some good for those families. It was only later, back in Washington, as part of a Congressional briefing, that I watched nearly an hour of real-time footage of the attacks and the enormity of the horror landed on me. Afterward, I had to sit in my office for half an hour, alone, silent, and still. To this day, I cannot erase from my head the images of the mutilated bodies, dismembered teenagers, and burned-down kibbutzim.

Jewish-Americans reacted to the terror on October 7 with shock and despair. The concept of Israel as the ultimate shelter for Jews was shattered that morning, replaced again by that feeling of dread—familiar to Jews across two millennia—that indiscriminate violence against Jews could happen anywhere.

On an unspoken level, we expected to see the world's empathy, an outpouring of support and solidarity with the Jewish state of Israel—and from most corners of American society, we did. The unprovoked mass slaughter of Israeli civilians and the rape of Israeli women were condemned by people of goodwill everywhere. But amazingly, a few corners of American society did not condemn the attack. Instead, long before any significant Israeli military response, they held pro-Palestinian rallies, where protesters appeared to celebrate the murders.

It would take only a week for protesters to start gathering outside my offices in Midtown Manhattan and Upstate New York, and my home in Brooklyn, to chant a variation on the refrain, familiar to anyone who has followed the anti-Israel protests since October 7: "Schumer, Schumer, you can't hide, you're supporting genocide." I wished that I could go down there and reason with them. To explain why that charge against Israel is false, and why it's so cutting. To discuss the complexities of the region, and how I was working with our government to pressure Israel to limit civilian casualties, increase humanitarian assistance to Gaza, and bring the hostages home. How the situation was made far more difficult because Hamas was using Palestinian civilians as human shields. But I refrained from doing so. Whenever I've tried to start a rational discussion with these protesters in private conversations, I've been shouted down, called names, and cursed at. They didn't want to have a discussion. Many seemed to exhibit the same absolutism that I encountered fifty years ago at Harvard, the same unwillingness to listen to any other side apart from their own.

Within a few weeks of October 7, Jews in America started getting attacked, verbally and physically, on street corners, outside synagogues, and on college greens. Within a few months, we started hearing comments like those made by a Columbia University student leader of the protest movement, who compared Zionists to white supremacists and Nazis. "These are all the same people," he said. "The existence of them and the projects they have built, i.e., Israel, it's all antithetical to peace. And so, yes, I feel very comfortable, very comfortable, calling for those people to die."

"Be grateful," he added, "that I'm not just going out and murdering Zionists." Unfortunately, these extreme remarks signaled a broader trend. Explicit calls for violence against Zionists—sometimes code for Israelis, sometimes code for Jews—have been repeated in many places and on college campuses no less.

By now it is clear: We have a problem with Israel-related antisemitism in America today. The initial lack of empathy by some after a brutal terrorist attack on Israeli soil opened our eyes. The sustained and increasing blame that Israel receives, far beyond what any other country would face when put in similar circumstances, alerted us to the threat. The attacks on Jews and Jewish life in the United States since October 7—often unrelated to Israel but on Jewish students, teachers, community and religious leaders, businesses and restaurants—convinced us that Israel-related antisemitism was a major issue. Antisemitism is a light sleeper; it only takes a nudge to wrest it from slumber. Once awake, it is liable to grow in intensity and could remain long after the war in Gaza is over.

Antisemitism driven by a critique of Israel is not an entirely new phenomenon. In 2009 and 2014, during prior conflicts between Israel and Hamas in Gaza, there was also a measurable rise in antisemitic incidents in the United States. But since October 7, we have entered a whole new world. In the first three months after the attack, there were as many explicitly antisemitic incidents in America as there were in the entire prior year, and 2023 would end with the highest number of antisemitic incidents recorded in the United States since the

ADL first started keeping records forty-five years ago. Similar data poured in from Europe and other countries around the globe.

The great rise of explicitly anti-Jewish sentiment in the United States after October 7 raises several serious questions about our understanding of Israel and how it is related to antisemitism. As a society, we must strive to answer them.

Does antisemitism fuel criticism of Israel? And does criticism of Israel, when it is exaggerated, venomous, and inaccurate, fuel antisemitism?

What elements of the current debate about Israel as a country are antisemitic, or contain shades of antisemitism? And, on the other hand, when is criticism of Israel not antisemitic at all?

Is anti-Zionism—the rejection of the Jewish right to a state of their own in their ancestral homeland of Israel—a version of antisemitism?

What words or slogans, used intentionally or not, should be avoided?

Just where exactly is the line to be drawn?

As a country, we need to have an honest conversation about where the boundaries lie even with due consideration to First Amendment rights; where legitimate criticism of Israel ends, and antisemitism begins. It is not an easy conversation to have. There are very strong feelings involved and decades of messy political, diplomatic, and military history. These questions are morally complex and require people to hold conflicting thoughts in their heads. But it is important for Americans to understand the Jewish-American perspective on Israel, and why certain criticisms are, and why they feel like, direct attacks on the Jewish people as a whole. Not everyone will agree with my definitions or feelings. But in order to form a better understanding of how the existence of Israel and the war in Gaza are producing increasing antisemitism in the United States, we must try to unravel the knot.

IT MUST BE said, clearly and from the start, that anyone can criticize the policies of Israel's government, the actions of its military, the statements of its politicians, and denounce the devastating loss of life in Gaza without exhibiting a shred of antisemitism. By no means is Israel a perfect nation. The country's government is not and must not be beyond reproach. Anyone, Jewish or non-Jewish, who automatically equates even the slightest criticism of Israel's actions with antisemitism is flatly wrong. Worse, that person makes it even harder to have a constructive dialogue about these emotional and complex issues.

One could list many potential criticisms of Israel's government, its domestic policies, and its foreign relations that are not at all antisemitic. I might disagree with some of those criticisms. I might find some of them unfair or lacking in context. But it is perfectly legitimate, and not remotely antisemitic, to question the conduct of an ally nation—although the criticism can be made more effective when care is taken to understand its history and an attempt is made to understand that nation's perspective.

If all criticism of Israel fell into this category, there would be no need for this chapter. But too much of the recent criticism leveled at Israel isn't about its recent policies or actions, but rather more fundamental questions about its very existence.

Many of these characterizations do fall under the umbrella of antisemitism, and it's crucial to understand what they are and why.

THE DEFINITION OF antisemitism that was developed by the International Holocaust Remembrance Alliance in 2016, adopted or endorsed since by forty-five countries, and used by our State Department as a guideline, lists the following as illustrative examples of antisemitism related to Israel:

- Accusing the Jews as a people, or Israel as a state, of inventing or exaggerating the Holocaust.
- Accusing Jewish citizens of being more loyal to Israel, or to the alleged priorities of Jews worldwide, than to the interests of their own nations.
- Denying the Jewish people their right to self-determination, e.g., by claiming that the existence of a State of Israel is a racist endeavor.
- Applying double standards by requiring of Israel a behavior not expected or demanded of any other democratic nation.
- Using the symbols and images associated with classic antisemitism (e.g., claims of Jews killing Jesus or blood libel) to characterize Israel or Israelis.
- Drawing comparisons of contemporary Israeli policy to that of the Nazis.
- Holding Jews collectively responsible for actions of the state of Israel.

Some of these definitions are more universally accepted than others. In my experience, only a few on the extremes compare current Israeli policy to that of the Nazis or claim that Israel invented or exaggerated the Holocaust. I think few would dispute those notions to be antisemitic. The other categories, however, require more exploration into the ways in which criticism of Israel veers into antisemitism. We can find examples of each in recent history as well as in contemporary debates about Israel, where actions against Jews and language at rallies and protests all too often fall under these definitions.

Over the seventy-six-plus years since Israel's creation, there have been hardened antisemites and antisemitic regimes that have used the country—and its Jewish character—as both a vehicle for and a target of their antisemitism. In the Soviet Union, for instance, Stalin developed a virulently anti-Zionist plank in the Communist Party platform. Through propaganda and official policy, the Soviet Union's hostility to Israel mirrored the repression of its own Jewish citizens. Soviet Jews were barred until 1971 from emigrating to Israel. Historians of the period, including Howard Sachar, describe Soviet anti-Zionism as explicitly antisemitic, couched in historical antisemitic tropes. Israel's victory in the 1967 Six-Day War was attributed to an "all-powerful international force" by Soviet propagandists; antisemites have often described Israel's power, and sometimes America's support for the Jewish state, as evidence of Jewish domination over world affairs. Referring to Israel's success whether in the military or the economic realm as an emblem or proof of an international Jewish conspiracy is explicitly antisemitic.

Another clear-cut example of antisemitism is when it is

assumed that Jews everywhere have a greater loyalty to Israel than to the country in which they live. It harkens back to the age-old antisemitic trope of dual loyalty, the idea that Jews are not as American as their fellow citizens because they hold a secret allegiance to Israel. The same trope dogged Catholics in America for decades as nativist Protestants claimed they would be loyal to the Pope and not to the American Republic. This prejudice led to crosses being burned in the South to greet Al Smith's presidential campaign train in 1928 and required candidate John F. Kennedy to give a major speech to the Greater Houston Ministerial Association, a group of Protestant ministers, on the issue of his religion in 1960.

A variation on this theme is that every Jew must be a supporter of Israel, simply because they are Jewish. This book has already included several recent examples of Jews being attacked or vilified for this presumption. The director of the Brooklyn Museum, whose apartment building was smeared with red paint, and who was called a "white supremacist Zionist." The Jewish deli on the Upper East Side of New York that was vandalized with graffiti of a swastika. The falafel shop in Philadelphia that was targeted by a protest rally for no other reason except that the proprietor is Israeli-American. There have been numerous other examples, and we can be unequivocal in condemning these overtly antisemitic attacks. To hold every Jew collectively responsible for every action of the Israeli government is antisemitism, plain and simple.

To me, some of the most heartbreaking incidents involve Jewish students and Jewish children: bullied, ostracized, or attacked at school or on campus. During a girls' high school basketball game in my home state of New York last January, players from Leffell, a private Jewish day school, were on the receiving end of antisemitic slurs. According to the New York City Public Schools Alliance, a player on the opposing team said, "I support Hamas, you fucking Jew." She said this to a seventeen-year-old girl who goes to school in Hartsdale, New York. Imagine her confusion, her fear, and her undeserved shame. What does a junior point guard from Westchester County have to do with what's happening in the Gaza Strip? This kind of comment is becoming all too frequent in post–October 7 America.

Regrettably, some of the most extreme rhetoric against Israel and, by extension, its current government and citizens, has led some of the more militant and ignorant protesters to attack Jewish people simply because they are Jewish. Everyone in America, regardless of their views on the state of Israel, should recognize that this is clearly and unambiguously antisemitic.

CRITICAL TO UNDERSTANDING the relationship between antisemitism and Israel is the concept of the double standard. Applying a double standard to Jews is a form of discrimination and one of the ways that the world has always practiced antisemitism. Jewish history is replete with chapters during which our people were forced to live by a different set of rules and expectations than everyone else. Abba Eban said to the protesters in the gallery in my college auditorium: Everyone could be a farmer, but not the Jew. Everyone could live in Moscow, but not the Jew. These are universally accepted as examples of antisemitism. I feel, as Ambassador Eban did, that it is equally antisemitic to celebrate every people gaining statehood except for the Jew. To say the only people in the world who are not entitled to their own state are the Jews. To me, that is indisputably antisemitic. I believe the vast majority of Jews would strongly agree with this sentiment.

This issue is very important to understanding antisemitism in America and its relationship to Israel. From the time Israel was founded, Jews have always felt that we were being discriminated against when it came to self-determination. That there was a deep undercurrent of unfairness and prejudice when people denied the Jewish people the right to aspire to a national homeland when almost all others were encouraged to establish theirs. That is how it felt to us when we read about the internationally organized boycotts against Israel and about biased resolutions targeting Israel that were routinely pushed at the United Nations. We wonder: *Why is Israel the one country in the world whose elimination is most openly called for? Even when people totally disagree with the actions of other countries, no one questions their right to have a state. No one asks the Russians to defend Russian statehood, or the Hungarians, or the Cambodians for that matter.*

But fortunately, for most of Israel's existence, when the vast majority of the world denied Israel's right to exist, America defended it, and the vast majority of Americans felt that it was a good thing the Jews had achieved a state of their own. In recent years, however, and especially after October 7, the idea that the Jewish people do not deserve a homeland has regained renewed prominence among some in America. In certain corners, people now feel that it is acceptable to question Israel's claim to nationhood. Many feel justified chanting "From the river to the sea, Palestine will be free," which includes the entire geographic area of Israel. That chant suggests the same opinion: that there should be no Israel, raising the specter of the double standard.

There is another element to questioning Israel's right to exist, which goes beyond unfairness and even prejudice. There is the practical matter of what happens to the seven million Jews living in Israel, half of all the Jews in the world, if the country were to be wiped from the map. Openly proposing an end to Israel raises distressing questions about the safety of the Jews residing there today. When Hamas calls for the elimination of Israel, we can presume they are calling for the elimination or at least the forced removal of at least half of the world's Jews. When radical groups chant the slogan "From the river to the sea," do they know they are quoting from the Hamas charter? Do they know the charter calls for the expulsion of Jews from Israel in the name of Palestinian liberation, and even suggests that all Jews in Israel be killed? That is why when Jewish-Americans hear the suggestion that there should be no Israel "from the river to the sea," there is a very real sense that antisemitism is at work.

The use of the terms "Zionist" and "Zio" as a slander, insult, or curse word—now commonplace among the anti-Israel protest community—is another way that some express total opposition to Israel's right to exist. "Smash the Zionist settler state." "Zionism is racism." When those terms are used as epithets for all Jews, that is wrong and is blatantly antisemitic; like when someone yells "you fucking Zionist" when what they really mean to say is "you fucking Jew." But also, when the term "Zionism," the basis for Israel's existence, is repeatedly used as a slur, it has another consequence. It delegitimizes the entire state of Israel, once again invoking the double standard.

Equating Zionism with "racism" achieves the same effect. It cuts to the core of Israel's existence and has long been used to delegitimize Israel as a national project. When other peoples seek their nationhood, is that racist? Why only the Jews? There is nothing about believing in the need for a Jewish homeland that is inherently racist, just as there is nothing contradictory about being a Zionist and supporting Palestinian statehood alongside Israeli statehood. Indeed, that is exactly what many Jewish-American Zionists believe. But the charge of "Zionism is racism" continues to cast a long shadow over Israel. The crux of this issue was tackled by one of my role models in politics, Senator Daniel Patrick Moynihan, who held the other Senate seat in New York when I was first elected and was one of the leading orators and intellectuals in American politics for much of the second half of the twentieth century. As our ambassador to the United Nations in 1975, he famously stood up against a biased UN resolution that declared that "Zionism is a form of racism and racial discrimination." The resolution was pushed by the powerful Arab bloc at the UN, and the vast majority of nations went along. Moynihan was nearly alone in speaking out against it. Moynihan bravely called out the "Zionism is racism" campaign for what it was: a tool used by Israel's opponents designed to invalidate the idea of a Jewish state. In his speech, he described how the campaign to label Zionism as racism was a way to give "the abomination of antisemitism," quoting that year's Nobel Peace Laureate, "the appearance of international sanction."

Israel was formed *because of* antisemitism, because antisemitism in Nazi Germany nearly extinguished European Jewry. To routinely and openly question the very existence of that nation—founded to give Jewish life a second chance, to give Jews a place to escape antisemitism—for me, and many Jewish-Americans, crosses the line. Especially when Israel is the only country on the receiving end of that question.

ON SOME WEEKEND mornings, over the din of faraway sirens, the screech of tires, and the usual sounds of the city, I can hear the bullhorn shouts of the small group of protesters who continue to meet outside my apartment in Brooklyn. The chant accusing me of supporting a genocide is by far the most common—"Schumer, Schumer, you can't hide..."—but there are others, too. There are signs that accuse Israel of being a white supremacist state, and a "settler-colonialist" nation. While I am a public figure, and this kind of activity comes with the territory, I often think about how other Jewish-Americans are processing the explosion of these terms into our national conversation. What are we to make of those claims? The rush to label Israel guilty of a genocide? The accusation that Jews do not and have never belonged in Israel, but rather settled it, like hated European conquistadors?

To the vast majority of Jewish-Americans, the accusation of genocide is the most painful, cruel, unfair, and vicious. I feel that unfairness quite strongly, not only because I believe it does not describe what is happening in Gaza but because of the history of my own family.

Genocide is officially defined as the deliberate and systematic destruction, in whole or in part, of a national, ethnic, racial, or religious group. It occurs when it is the policy, and subsequent actions of a state, to eliminate a specific group because of their national, ethnic, racial, or religious background. Whatever one's view of how the war in Gaza was conducted, it is not and has never been the policy of the Israeli government to exterminate the Palestinian people. The Israel-Gaza war was not the unprovoked slaughter of Palestinians, purely to wipe them out as a people. It was a military response to a terrorist attack on Israeli soil, perpetrated by a terrorist group, Hamas, which does indeed advocate the genocide of the Jews in Israel, and acted on that impulse on October 7.

For Israelis, October 7 was their country's version of 9/11, except instead of the perpetrators living half a world away, they lived just across Israel's border. The hundreds of hostages in captivity reminded Israelis, daily, of the trauma of the original attack. Would other nations not be expected to respond with military force?

The Jewish people have experienced a genocide, systematic and on an industrial scale, unlike any in world history in its scope and cruelty. This undoubtedly informs how we think, see, and feel about the use of the term. The renowned British historian Simon Schama, in a talk last summer at Aspen Ideas, refuted the charge that Israel was committing genocide in Gaza by recounting the worst chapters from the Holocaust, which demonstrate the massive scale at which the Nazis operated. During the first week of the Nazi occupation of Kyiv, in September 1941, the Jews of the city were summoned to a quiet ravine just outside the city. They were forced to strip naked and enter the ravine, and were then shot in small groups: In just two days, 33,771 Jews were murdered at Babyn Yar. The Nazis soon discovered that firing squads were not efficient enough. By July 1944, 20,000 Jews were routinely being killed in the gas chambers of Auschwitz daily. And in November 1943, in what was called Operation "Harvest Festival," 43,000 were shot to death at labor camps in Majdanek, Trawniki, and Poniatowa in Poland over the course of just more than a single day—the largest single massacre of Jews by Germans during the Holocaust.

The Holocaust emerged from the desire to wipe out an entire people who the Nazis did not see as fellow humans. It need not be stated, but the decision to round up and murder six million Jews was not in response to them attacking Germany, but rather was done with malice aforethought, design, and meticulous planning. At the Wannsee Conference in 1942, high-ranking security officers in the Nazi regime met to coordinate the "Final Solution to the Jewish Question," after having seen that early experiments with gas chambers and crematoria could be a more effective way of dealing with the eleven million Jews living in Europe. It wasn't long after the Conference that a network of extermination camps was established, including five in the calendar year after the meeting at Wannsee. In 1933, before the Nazi regime came to power, there were 9.5 million Jews living in Europe. By 1950, some years after the end of the Holocaust, there were 3.5 million Jews. Two out of every three Jews in Europe (one out of three Jews in the world) were slaughtered, purposefully, by a regime that assembled a continent-sized machinery to speed the process.

While the number of victims is not material to the definition, the fact that the Holocaust did, in living memory, nearly wipe out the Jewish population of Europe makes the charge of genocide against Israel that much more brutally unfair. The term "genocide" has a specific meaning and carries historical and emotional weight, not just for the protesters shouting it but for Jews in America, many of whom are descendants of the victims of the twentieth century's worst genocide. The word "genocide" entered our lexicon, in fact, because a Polish Jewish jurist named Raphael Lemkin coined it to describe the crimes of the Holocaust. For those of us whose relations perished in the Holocaust, hearing Israel and Jewish supporters of Israel being accused of genocide is vicious. Even for the small number of Jews who have no family history connected to the Holocaust, it's extremely painful.

Like most Americans, I read the daily reports of civilian casualties caused by Israeli bombing. Not nearly enough care has been taken to prevent the loss of innocent lives. As the war has gone on, Israel's military campaign has also reportedly shut off the corridor's access to critical resources and created desperate poverty in Gaza. In my judgment, Israel has gone much too far in its overly stringent inspection and restriction of humanitarian assistance that must cross the border between Israel and Gaza, including food, water, and medical supplies. While the Israeli government is concerned that Hamas is capturing the resources to support its terrorist activities, the restrictions are causing an all-too-high loss of life.

Those actions can be condemned, but they do not constitute a genocide under any fair definition. Calling these actions genocidal is also counterproductive. It makes it much harder to convince the Israeli government to adopt changes, which is the fervent desire of many, if not most, Jewish-Americans and those of us in power who have sought to surge humanitarian assistance into the region.

THOSE WHO HURL the charge of genocide at Israel ignore another very important factor that has caused such a high number of civilian casualties in Gaza: the tactics of Hamas.

By committing such heinous atrocities on October 7 before sneaking its entire leadership and military wing back into tunnels, and hiding among the civilian population in hospitals, schools, and refugee camps in Gaza, Hamas knew it was inviting an immense civilian toll during the war. These tactics are not new. Hamas routinely places the rockets it fires at Israel near or inside schools, mosques, churches, and hospitals. Their military structures are embedded inside heavily residential areas of the Gaza Strip. So, when Israel tries to eliminate rocket sites or military targets—as any country would do in response to rocket attacks on its territory—civilians are killed. It is almost part of Hamas's military doctrine that Gaza's civilians are assets to be exploited, even if they are killed in the process. Messages obtained by the *Wall Street Journal* this past summer reveal that the late military leader of Hamas, Yahya Sinwar, believed that more fighting and more civilian casualties in Gaza were to his advantage, calling them "necessary sacrifices."

Too many news agencies and newspapers ignore these facts. They give Hamas a pass by failing to regularly discuss the shameful practice of using innocent Gazans as human shields, which is central to their fighting strategy. I believe the loss of innocent Palestinian life should be covered extensively by the media, and it is. But media reports almost always leave out how the tactics of Hamas are at least partially responsible for many of these deaths. Downplaying or ignoring the role of Hamas while keeping a watchful eye on the deaths and despair caused by Israel has consequences. I believe it has led to an inaccurate perception of the harsh realities of this war and made it easier for those who claim "genocide" to do so. When I have been able to talk to pro-Palestinian protesters in an earnest attempt to bridge our divide, I ask them about Hamas's role in this catastrophic war, and especially its gross disregard for its own people. They inevitably do not answer and seem totally unwilling to acknowledge these realities.

When it comes to Israel, critics are quick to equate an alarming loss of life to genocide, but often fail to do it when this occurs in other parts of the world. In the Darfur region of Sudan, for instance, an estimated 200,000 Black African tribal people were targeted and killed by the Sudanese government and nomad Arab militia forces in the early 2000s. In Syria, Israel's next-door neighbor, more than half a million civilians have died, most of them at the hands of Bashar al-Assad's monstrous regime. Where were the protesters calling for an end to the suffering of a population more than ten times the size of Gaza's, over more than twelve brutal years? Where are the mass demonstrations in front of the Chinese embassy and Chinese-owned businesses over China's persecution of the eleven million Uyghurs? Why only Israel? The word "genocide"—most painful to Jewish ears—is almost never used in these many other instances. To most Jews, it stings of the double standard—that *only* the Jewish state is singled out for this particularly noxious term.

Many may dispute the idea that it is antisemitic to criticize Israel for certain actions when you are not criticizing other states who do the same or worse. There is some merit to that argument, but when it comes to the particular word "genocide," with how wrongly it is applied and with all its freighted baggage, I believe it is not.

I hope more people take a moment to understand the context, definition, and gravity of the charge before accusing Israel of a genocide, or Jews in America for supporting one, especially given the history of the Jewish people. It creates the impression that Israel is monstrous, and therefore Jewish supporters of Israel might be monsters, too. Antisemitism, once again, could lie just around the bend.

ANOTHER TERM THAT seems unfair to many Jews is when Israel is labeled a "settler-colonial state." Terms like "imperialist"—as the PLP-SDS called it when I was in college—or "white supremacist Zionists" are also used to describe its inhabitants. These labels have long confounded me. It's hard to be a white supremacist nation when most of the voting population is not white. According to a legal definition of settler-colonialism, it is "a system of oppression...that aims to displace the population of a nation (oftentimes indigenous people) and replace it with a settler population." In scholarship, a classic example pertains to the displacement and extermination of Native tribes in North

America with the arrival of European settlers. But the Jewish experience in Israel could not be more different. Jews can trace their roots to the land of Israel for many thousands of years and have lived there for just as long. It's where the Jewish people originated and where our first temples were built, only to be destroyed by invaders. Jewish people through the centuries have looked to Israel as their homeland, not as a place where they could extract resources and exploit whoever was living there at the time. When Israel was founded, Jews came to build a nation, improve the land, and live there permanently, as well as escape the antisemitism they had faced for hundreds of years in other parts of the world.

Many of those who use the term "settler-colonialist" for Israel believe it is validated by what happened to the 700,000 Palestinians who fled or were expelled from their homes between December 1947 and March 1949, in what Palestinians refer to as the "Nakba"—the "catastrophe." It is important to know the history around these events.

In November 1947, the United Nations passed a resolution partitioning Palestine to create *two states* between the river and the sea, Jewish and Arab. It is true that it was expected that Palestinians living within the designated boundaries of the Jewish state would move to the Arab state, just as it became clear that the 850,000 Jews who'd been living in Arab countries for generations would also have to move. (Under the plan, Jerusalem, under international control, would be an equal mix of Jews and Arabs.) Jews living for generations in those Arab nations had their property confiscated, their lives threatened, and the vast majority of them were essentially expelled over the next two decades. Some 650,000 of them chose to settle in Israel, and their descendants form a large part of the Israeli population. They were not white settler-colonists, but Middle Eastern refugees seeking a safe place to live.

Over the coming decades, Israel absorbed and integrated the displaced Jewish people of Arab lands, but the Arab nations, vehemently opposed to the creation of Israel, demanded the United Nations set up refugee camps for the Palestinians. They didn't recognize the right to a Jewish state, believing instead that it should be wiped out. When Israel was destroyed, they imagined, the refugees could all return. Today, it seems forgotten that the refugee camps were created by the Arab rulers at the time and not the state of Israel.

For more than two thousand years, Jews were stateless, forced to move endlessly from country to country, hoping each time that we would be treated better upon arrival. History is full of chapters in which populations have been made to adapt, integrate, assimilate, or sometimes move to nearby countries. As the late-night TV host Bill Maher put it, in a telling segment in December 2023, "Things change. Countries. Boundaries. Empires. Palestine was under the Ottoman Empire for 400 years but today an Ottoman is something you put under your feet. Was it unjust that even a single Arab family was forced to move upon the founding of the Jewish state? Yes. But it's also not rare. Happening all through history, all over the world. And mostly what people do is make the best of it.... Kosovo was the cradle of Christian Serbia. Then it became Muslim. They fought a war about it in the nineties. But stopped. They didn't keep it going for seventy-five years." To most Israeli Jews, the demand by Palestinians for the "right of return" and for the full territory of

Israel to be part of a single Palestinian state is unreasonable, a madness that dooms two distrustful populations to perpetually hold knives to each other's throats. It's a madness that not only thwarts Palestinian aspirations for a true state of their own but keeps many Palestinians in poverty.

The two-state solution—a Jewish state and a Palestinian state living side by side in peace—has long been championed by American presidents, and in recent decades, several Israeli prime ministers have also engaged in talks and negotiations designed to advance the cause of Palestinian statehood. In the early 1990s, Prime Minister Yitzhak Rabin and PLO chairman Yasser Arafat took part in the Oslo peace process that led to the creation of the Palestinian Authority, allowing for limited self-governance by Palestinians in parts of the West Bank and Gaza Strip. In 1995, Rabin was tragically assassinated by a far-right Israeli five weeks after he signed the Oslo accords, and the peace process fell apart. In 2000, at Camp David, Prime Minister Ehud Barak put forward a proposal in which Israel accepted Palestinian sovereignty over all of the Gaza Strip and 91 percent of the West Bank. That proposal was rejected by Arafat. In 2008, PM Ehud Olmert in a private meeting with Mahmoud Abbas, the Palestinian Authority president since Arafat's demise, made an offer described as the most far-reaching one ever made by an Israeli prime minister to a Palestinian leader. Again, it was rejected.

After this series of rejections, the Israeli public began to lose faith in the hope of a two-state solution, turning instead to politicians like Netanyahu who promised merely security, rather than security through peace.

The history in the region makes it clear that the Jewish state of Israel is not a settler-colonialist nation. The land was populated by Jews long before it was founded. It became a land of safety for Jewish refugees from Europe after the Holocaust and from the Arab world at the time of its creation. It endorsed and endeavored to abide by international plans for the partition of the land between Arabs and Jews, and once that plan was rejected by the Arabs, it tried on several occasions to establish a separate peace. And yet Israel is treated, unfairly and incorrectly, as if it has never believed in Palestinian statehood.

You may be asking yourself, *What do these decades of Middle Eastern history have to do with antisemitism?* To me it is clear-cut. When inflammatory charges like "genocide" and "settler-colonialism" and "Zionism is racism" are hurled against Israel, it epitomizes the double standard that has been the core of antisemitism for centuries. In addition, the hatred and negativity it generates gets applied to Jewish supporters of Israel in America, and sometimes to all Jews. This is not supposition; it is the most direct explanation for the dramatic rise in antisemitic abuse, harassment, and violence against Jews in America and why it occurred after October 7.

I have tried to elucidate Jewish and Israeli history to help determine which criticisms of Israel are antisemitic and which exacerbate antisemitism and which do not. My answers are not going to be everyone's answers, but trying to ascertain the line of demarcation is maybe the only way to prevent surging antisemitism from growing worse.

Of course, the accusation of "antisemitism" itself should not be tossed around lightly. Just because Israel is the only Jewish state in the world doesn't mean that it cannot be held responsible or accountable. Just because most Jewish-Americans feel that holding Israel to a double standard is unacceptable doesn't mean that Israel should be held to no standard at all.

Just as important, we must be careful not to permanently condemn as an antisemite every single person who might use language that many Jewish-Americans consider over the line. Many have little idea of what these slogans, phrases, and words imply; what they entail; and how dangerous they can be. If left unrefuted, these slogans can lead to a more virulent and dangerous form of antisemitism. It's our obligation to rebut them.

ISRAEL HAS ALWAYS had its detractors in the United States, including those critical weeks of debate in the Truman White House before it drew its infant breath. But despite the presence of those early antagonists, America has been unlike most other nations in the world in its support for the Jewish state of Israel. America was Israel's first and most important friend—and remains so. Israel, for its part, is America's only democratic partner in a region dominated by tyranny and fanaticism. It remains, too, a land of last resort for Jews around the world fleeing persecution and antisemitism. While Jews in America have lived a very different story of generational progress than Jews in Israel, our destinies are intertwined. It is hard to imagine the creation and survival of the Jewish state of Israel if not for America, and the Jews in America are naturally linked to Israel. Israel has been not only a source of Jewish-American pride, but a country where our history, heritage, and often many of our relatives reside.

Over eight decades, through multiple wars and existential crises, the special relationship between the United States and

Israel was unwavering, and helped the Jewish state survive and prosper. It has also been a source of identity and hope for the Jewish people. But if antisemitism and double standards against Israel become more prevalent here in America, that vital relationship is at risk.

CHAPTER 10

CONCLUSION

I have always imagined the Jewish people as having placed two bets for our future in the modern world. Both began with long odds. As antisemitism was rising in Europe in the latter half of the nineteenth century, Jews began to fear for their safety in the capitals and countryside of the old continent. Chastened by history, some felt that only a nation for Jews was sufficient to ward off the ultimate danger, and the Zionist movement was born. Those early Zionists placed a bet on an imaginary country: an ancient homeland made anew—Israel—a dream realized only after the Jewish people emerged from a waking nightmare. The second bet was made by millions of immigrants who vaulted forth to a new promised land—America—where they hoped, by diving into the stream of openness and tolerance that coursed through that land of opportunity, they would find, and help forge, a very different kind of Zion. Remarkably, both of those bets came good. Today, nearly 90 percent of the world's Jews live in either America or Israel.

In these two national projects, Jews believed they had found the antidote to historical antisemitism. On the one hand, a country where the regime could never turn on the Jews because the regime itself was Jewish. On the other, a country whose national virtues and natural instincts made true assimilation possible, even if there were frictions from time to time. The United States was a nation where you could be, impossibly and yet without contradiction, 100 percent Jewish and 100 percent American at the same time. Jews and Jewish identity became so integrated into the fabric of America that it was hard to tell where one stopped and the other began. Jews believed that we had found in America a country that stood outside and beyond history, the great exception to the rule, where Jewish life kept getting better and safer, richer and more varied. "History is a nightmare from which I am trying to awake," wrote James Joyce about the turn of the twentieth century, his protagonist in *Ulysses* longing to move past centuries of Irish oppression, religious dogmatism, and British colonial rule. In America, Jews found the country of Joyce's dream for our own diaspora, a place where we could finally wake up from history.

The questions that now linger in my mind are the same questions that led me to write this book: How long can such a country last? How long will such a country last? What must we do to ensure that it does?

We have seen antisemitism infect the most extreme corners of both major political movements in America. Many mainstream politicians and leaders have not been alert enough to the danger nor bold enough in calling it out. Social media has

CONCLUSION

exposed more Americans to violent, extreme, and conspiratorial antisemitism than ever before. Global catastrophes in the first part of the twenty-first century have driven misinformation and confusion about, and sometimes animus toward, Jews. As the Middle East remains embroiled in conflict, the complicated relationship between anti-Israeli, anti-Zionist, and antisemitic sentiments will continue to be problematic. In the eighty years since the end of the Holocaust, the memory of that historical trauma has faded, replaced in the minds of too many young Americans by doubt about its veracity and extent, or else a limited awareness of the events at all. This is a period of growing and serious threat. For the first time in my life, I have felt the specter of antisemitism haunting the American continent, this land that has been our most cherished escape from history.

Believing there is great value in a warning, I have tried to sound an alarm. I have tried to tackle the specific factors that have made people more likely to be antisemitic or susceptible to antisemitism at this moment in time. I have also tried to describe a deeper historical truth: that centuries upon centuries of prejudice have created a societal reservoir of antisemitism, a poisoned wellspring that can be tapped, drawn from, and swallowed by people living in all times and in all places. American society must understand and grapple with both if it is to overcome the antisemitism we see today.

I do believe that if we meaningfully address the recent factors contributing to the rise of antisemitism in America, we will see fewer incidents and expressions of it. If we find an appropriate balance in the regulation of social media, for example, we can reduce the spread of misinformation and hatred while respecting the First Amendment and retaining the technology's manifold benefits. If we successfully pressure political leaders to denounce all forms of bigotry, but particularly in their own political movements where it will be most effective, I believe racist and antisemitic feelings are more likely to remain on the far extremes. If we start to rebuild the social and moral bonds in our country that have recently frayed, and if we bring greater stability and prosperity to our country, I suspect there will be less fear and anxiety, and fewer people will feel an impulse to find an "other" to blame. Those are all incredibly noble goals, and though hard to attain, we should pursue them, regardless of their effect on Jews or antisemitism. And yet, even if all those things came to pass, I'm not sure the danger would completely disappear. While fewer triggers would lower the risk of antisemitism in American society, I do not believe that it would expunge it.

"Nature herself," feared Montaigne, "attaches to man some instinct for inhumanity." Racism, bigotry, and prejudice: these evils have always been with us, our great shame as a species, one of our greatest challenges to overcome. Antisemitism is one of those sins. It is about denying the humanity of Jews, who are not only a religious group but a nation of people. So, while we must address the circumstances and ideas and technologies that cause it to flare up, the only way to truly make antisemitism subside is to educate people about it. To teach people its causes. To warn them about its effects. To link arms with people of goodwill everywhere to fight back. To describe what it means to be Jewish today and invite more people to learn about our heritage. To insist, again and again, on our common humanity.

We draw these lessons from our history and our religious traditions. "And you shall teach your children [this story]," begins a commandment from the Haggadah, which lays out the order of the Passover service. One of the themes of Passover is that Jews must fight the possibility of future enslavement by teaching the next generation about our deliverance and the meaning of liberty for all people. The Hebrew word Haggadah itself means "telling." On Purim, whenever the name of the Jew-hating Haman is said aloud, we are taught to spin or shake a wooden noisemaker called a grogger to blot out his name. My grandson Noah loves this part the most, even if he's not old enough yet to understand why we're doing it. There is a simple wisdom in this tradition, too. It is our job not only to teach, but to drown out the antisemite, to be louder than their hatred.

Modernity has reinforced this ancient wisdom. In the bleak years of shock and recovery after the Holocaust, a strategy emerged for how the Jewish people and its allies would counter the threat of antisemitism. Again, we would insist on teaching the events and the lessons of the Holocaust to future generations. Education, awareness, and memory: These were the watchwords. "Never again" summed up their purpose. Holocaust survivors traveled the world, forcing themselves to relive the unimaginable horror of their experiences in classrooms and conference halls because they believed it was their duty to bear witness and provide testimony. *The Diary of Anne Frank* became a fixture of middle and high school curricula. Museums, memorials, and monuments were raised in capitals and cities around the world. Whenever I visit the Holocaust Memorial Museum in our nation's capital, and see dozens of jabbering schoolchildren from every corner of the country, I am heartened that people are still learning, still being sensitized to the threats that Jews have faced. Just because misinformation on the internet and social media have made the job of teaching the truth of this historical trauma—and indeed many historical traumas—much harder, that doesn't mean the original effort was ill-conceived. In fact, the wide reach of the internet provides an opportunity to teach about Jewish history and the Holocaust in novel and creative ways. If anything, we have to find new ways to teach our history and, knowing that the generations that survived the Holocaust will someday pass from the earth, new ways to bear witness and provide testimony.

We can and must do a better job clarifying exactly what antisemitism is and what it is not. The more adeptly Americans can identify antisemitic themes, standards, and tropes, the most likely they are to avoid using them and prevent others around them from doing the same. We have to rekindle that instinct to instruct others, politely but passionately and persuasively, about the threat of antisemitism.

These pages are my own attempt to do so.

"WHITHER GOEST THOU, America, in thy shiny car in the night?" wondered a friend of the main character in Jack Kerouac's *On the Road*. I wonder, too, what direction our country is headed. Are these recent years of rising antisemitism merely a blip, an anomaly in the long story of Jewish progress in America? Or do they mark the beginning of a sea change? The end of the best time and best place in the history of the world to be Jewish.

While researching and writing this book, I have come across both dark chapters and golden ages, periods of discrimination and prejudice against Jews in America and periods of stunning progress—of not only growing acceptance but extraordinary achievement for Jewish-Americans. How do we reconcile America's amazing capacity for what has been a radical form of tolerance in world history with its instinct, too frequently, for the opposite? George Washington's letter to the Rhode Island synagogue in 1790 describes a nation where everyone, including the people of Abraham, should be able to sit under their own vine and fig tree, and there shall be none to make them afraid. Henry Ford, Father Coughlin, and the rallygoers at Madison Square Garden in 1939 would beg to differ. As long as Washington's idea of America has existed, there have been those competing notions. Today, as in every generation, there are people and politicians who believe that America is merely a nation of land and people, of soil and of blood, like many other nations. But from the very founding of our country, there have always been citizens and leaders who believe that America is more than that: that America is an idea, a set of values and principles—of liberty and equality, justice and opportunity. These fault lines continue to inform our politics today.

In that sense, antisemitism is not just a challenge for and about Jews. Antisemitism poses a challenge to the American project. Like other forms of racism and bigotry, it threatens our two-and-a-half-century experiment in a multiethnic, multicultural democracy. We are a nation conceived in liberty and dedicated to the proposition that all men and women are created equal. Antisemitism is the belief that some men and women are less equal than others; that some people's rights to life, liberty, and the pursuit of happiness are, in fact, alienable. Were antisemitism to become an acceptable part of modern

American discourse, it would threaten not only the safety and security of Jewish-Americans and other Americans, but the most fundamental and noble virtues of our country.

The recent rise of antisemitism is a test case for what kind of country we want to be, a summons to fight for the idea of America at her very best. Americans of all ages, colors, and creeds must renew the idea of our country as a large-hearted, open, and tolerant place. And despite some darkening clouds on the horizon, I remain deeply, unshakably hopeful that the best version of America will ultimately prevail.

I think about the improbability of my own family's journey, and how I got to where I am today. The Jewish-American story is fused in so many aspects of my life. While the name "Schumer" is derived from Hebrew, a legacy of our family's life in the Jewish ghettos of Eastern Europe, my parents gave me a middle name—Ellis, for Ellis Island—a reminder of how the Schumers came to be American, too. Inspired by that example, my wife, Iris, and I gave our second daughter the middle name "Emma," in honor of Emma Lazarus, the Jewish-American poet who wrote the timeless lines that now adorn the Statue of Liberty, a perfect distillation of the welcoming and tolerant America that gave our family the chance to grow and prosper and pass down more opportunities to our descendants than we ever imagined possible for ourselves.

> *"Give me your tired, your poor,*
> *Your huddled masses yearning to breathe free*
> *The wretched refuse of your teeming shore.*
> *Send these, the homeless, tempest-tost, to me,*
> *I lift my lamp beside the golden door!"*

Those lines, so resonant and inspiring to Americans today, were not always meant to sound that way. When they were written in 1883, they were not a description of the America that Emma Lazarus saw at the time but, rather, a vision of what she hoped America would become. She lived during a period of reactionary sentiment to the immigrants—including Italians, Greeks, and Russian Jews—who were arriving in droves on America's shores. Emma was then in her early thirties, writing poems and essays that spoke out against the persecution of Jews in Europe as well as growing antisemitism in the United States. One year earlier, the US Congress had passed the Chinese Exclusion Act of 1882—the first, but not the last, time that the United States would restrict immigration on the basis of national origin.

Today, we think of those words engraved on the pedestal as a reflection of America's spirit during an age of immigration and opportunity. But they were written as a hopeful protest, an expression of how Lazarus believed her fellow citizens *should* feel, rather than how many did at the time. She believed in the idea of a more welcoming country and spent much of her short life fighting for it. She insisted that America was something that it was not quite yet, but amazingly would become for much of the twentieth century. Alongside the efforts of many others, her words helped inspire a new national ethos, without which my family's story would not even be possible.

That is why I find her lines so inspiring. Not because they somehow predicted America's future, but because they remind me that whatever America's faults, we can always fashion our country into something better. We can refresh our national spirit. We can become more perfect. One hundred and forty-two years ago, her pen resting on a blank sheet of paper, Emma Lazarus was taking part in that boundless American project in which we are all now engaged: She was imagining what our country could, and ought, to be. A country, perhaps, where the Jewish son of an exterminator and a housewife could one day become the leader of the United States Senate.

"Isn't America a great country?" my grandmother Minnie asked Tip O'Neill on the day of my swearing in. I still believe in my bones that she was right.

ACKNOWLEDGMENTS

As a U.S. Senator, your day-to-day writing most often takes the form of a speech. Of the many differences between preparing a speech and writing a book (the greatest being the length of time it takes), one difference that stands out to me is that, in a speech, you typically acknowledge all the important people right at the outset. In a book, you must wait till the very end to express the enormous debt of gratitude that an author feels for everyone who helped bring it into the world. Don't let that fool you. Without the help of a very committed team of advisors, writers, and editors, and the support and guidance of friends and family, no effort like this would be possible.

The team at Hachette and Grand Central Publishing have been wonderful partners. Ben Sevier, Colin Dickerman, and Jimmy (not James) Franco have always believed in this book and endeavored to make it the best it could be, especially through Colin's consistently sharp and incisive edits. David Kuhn, my literary agent, first identified that my reflections on these topics could make a worthy contribution to the national conversation, and his team at Aevitas Creative Management helped guide this book into being. Alex Levy, a former aide of mine in the Senate and a resource to this day, lent his considerable knowledge and guidance to several different aspects of the project, from conception to promotion. Risa Heller, as well, deserves my thanks for her help with managing the many media responsibilities that come with publishing.

Along the way I have had a group of involved and interested readers whose reviews have sharpened my prose and sanded off some of the rougher edges: first and foremost, my wife, Iris, whose contributions are incomparable, but also my brother Bob and sister Fran; my daughters Alison and Jessica; my friends Carol Kellerman and Mark O'Donoghue; and Jimmy and Merryl Tisch. Some of these helpful readers scoured the text on not one but several occasions. Their time, effort, and brilliance are reflected throughout. Steve Barton, who has written with me speeches on antisemitism and the path forward in Israel and Gaza after October 7, also offered valuable suggestions and aided in the research and sourcing of background materials.

During the writing of the book, several friends and acquaintances reached out to provide helpful context, suggest research material, or simply to have an engaging discussion about what Americans can do to stop the rise of this prejudice, and all have helped shape my thinking. I want to thank Leonard Stern, Tom Freedman, George Pavlov, and especially Robert Kraft, whose Foundation to Combat Antisemitism is doing remarkable and hugely effective work to reduce antisemitism in the United States.

Josh Molofsky has been my writing partner for more than a decade, as my chief speechwriter in the Senate during several of the most important milestones in my career and some turbulent times in the history of our country. His willingness to work with me again on this project was one of the reasons—perhaps the decisive reason—that I believed I could accomplish the task alongside my normal schedule as a Senator. The fluency and emotional depth of these pages is a credit to his ability to bring both organization and poetry to my thoughts.

I have no greater thanks than to my family, whom I love so much and whose names, experiences, and suggestions can be found on page after page. To my daughters Alison and Jessica and their devoted spouses Biz and Mike: Thanks for being such willing counselors and sounding boards, even though you have very busy lives of your own. You have made your father prouder than you could ever imagine. My grandchildren, Noah, Eleanor, and Henry: You bring so much light into my life, and in many ways, you are who this book is for. My father, Abe, passed away a few years ago, but he left an indelible mark on my life. His life experiences and the lessons that he and my mom, Selma, taught me infuse many of the earlier chapters of the book. I love them both and miss my father still.

To my wife, Iris: Very simply, I could not have done this without you. Your memory of our family's history and the Jewish-American experience helped fill the book with wit and wisdom. Your careful review and edits brought clarity and brevity. On writing this book, and on everything else, you have always had my back.

SOURCES

Introduction

Exod. 3:1-12 (Shemot)

"2023 Hate Crime Statistics." Federal Bureau of Investigation, September 23, 2024.

"U.S. Antisemitic Incidents Skyrocketed 360% in Aftermath of Attack in Israel, According to Latest ADL Data." Anti-Defamation League, January 9, 2024.

Various California Jewish Organizations. Letter to the Office of the Secretary and Chief of Staff to the Regents Office of the Secretary and Chief of Staff to the Regents. "UC Regents Letter," March 15, 2024.

"Majority of American Jews Feel Less Safe after October 7 Hamas Terror Attack." American Jewish Committee, January 11, 2024.

Hill, J. Sellers, and Nia L. Orakwue. "Harvard Student Groups Face Intense Backlash for Statement Calling Israel 'entirely Responsible' for Hamas Attack." *The Harvard Crimson*, October 10, 2023.

O'Brien, Conor Cruise. *The Siege: The Saga of Israel and Zionism*. London: Faber & Faber, 2015.

Exod. 22:6-14 (Shemot)

Chapter 1. What Is Antisemitism

Zimmermann, Mosche. *Wilhelm Marr, the Patriarch of Antisemitism*. New York: Oxford University Press, 1986.

SOURCES

Marr, Wilhelm. *The Victory of Judaism Over Germanism*, 1879.

Oxford English Dictionary, s.v. "Semite (n.), sense 1."

Chapter 2. What Does It Mean to Be Jewish?

"What Is Shomrim?" NYPD Shomrim Society.

Weiner, Morris. "Three Jews Now Hold Four World Boxing Championships." *Jewish Telegraphic Agency*, June 17, 1934.

"'Titans of the Titanic': The Jewish Lower East Side's Mourning for Ida and Isidor Straus." The New York Public Library, April 3, 2023.

"Isidor and Ida Straus, Titanic Love Stories." Titanic Belfast.

Titanic. Twentieth Century Fox, 1997.

Ruth 1:16-17

Chapter 3. Antisemitism Throughout History

Gen. 37-50 (Bereshit)

Exod. 1:1-14:31 (Shemot)

Feldman, Louis H. *Studies in Hellenistic Judaism*. Leiden: Brill, 1996.

Josephus, Flavius. *Against Apion*

Esther 1-7

Horowitz, Elliott. *Reckless Rites: Purim and the Legacy of Jewish Violence*. Princeton, NJ: Princeton University Press, 2018.

Nirenberg, David. *Anti-Judaism: The Western Tradition*. New York: W.W. Norton & Co, 2014.

Johnson, Paul. *A History of the Jews*. New York: Harper Perennial, 1988.

Schama, Simon. *The Story of the Jews: Finding the Words, 1000 BC-1492 AD*. London: Bodley Head, 2013.

Schama, Simon. *Belonging: The Story of the Jews, 1492-1900*. London: Bodley Head, 2017.

Broadcast, *Columbus DNA, His True Origin*. Radiotelevisión Española, September 25, 2024.

Shakespeare, William. *The Merchant of Venice*.

Barzilay, Tzafrir. *Poisoned Wells: Accusations, Persecution, and Minorities in Medieval Europe, 1321-1422*. Philadelphia, PA: University of Pennsylvania Press, 2022.

Goebbels, Joseph. "The Jews Are Guilty!" Translated by Randall Bytwerk. German Propaganda Archive.

Weisman, Jonathan. "Robert F. Kennedy Jr. Airs Bigoted New Covid Conspiracy Theory About Jews and Chinese." *The New York Times*, July 15, 2023.

"Unraveling Anti-Semitic 9/11 Conspiracy Theories." Anti-Defamation League, 2003.

Horn, Dara. "Why the Most Educated People in America Fall for Anti-Semitic Lies." *The Atlantic*, February 15, 2024.

Gruen, Erich S. "Tacitus and the Defamation of the Jews." In *The Construct of Identity in Hellenistic Judaism: Essays on Early Jewish Literature and History*, 1st ed., 265–80. De Gruyter, 2016.

Sartre, Jean-Paul. *Anti-Semite and Jew*. New York: Schocken Books, 1965.

"Second Day, Wednesday, 11/21/1945, Part 04", in Trial of the Major War Criminals before the International Military Tribunal. Volume II. Proceedings: 11/14/1945-11/30/1945. [Official text in the English language.] Nuremberg: IMT, 1947. pp. 98-102.

Chapter 4. Antisemitism in America

Klier, John, and Shlomo Lambroza, eds. *Pogroms: Anti-Jewish Violence in Modern Russian History*. Cambridge University Press, 1992.

"Jewish Communities of Prewar Germany." United States Holocaust Memorial Museum.

N.H. Baynes, ed., *The Speeches of Adolf Hitler*, I, London, 1942, pp. 737-741

Herskowitz, Leo. "By Chance or Choice: Jews in New Amsterdam 1654." *American Jewish Archives Journal* 57, no. 1 & 2 (2005): 1-13

Soloveichik, Meir. *Adams, Jefferson, and the Jews: Supplementary Readings*. Yeshiva University, New York: The Straus Center for Torah and Western Thought, 2012.

"From John Adams to François Adriaan Van der Kemp, 31 December 1808," *Founders Online*, National Archives.

"From George Washington to the Hebrew Congregation in Newport, Rhode Island, 18 August 1790," *Founders Online*, National Archives.

Sarna, Jonathan, and Jonathan J Golden. Working paper. *The American Jewish Experience in the 20th Century*, 1999.

Josephson, Larry, Sarah Elzas, and Sara Porath. "No Dogs or Jews Allowed: The Story of Antisemitism in America." Episode. *Only in America: 350 Years of the American Jewish Experience*. Public Radio Exchange, April 20, 2007.

SOURCES

Wyman, David S. *The Abandonment of the Jews: America and the Holocaust, 1941–1945*. New York: Pantheon, 1984.

Fermaglich, Kirsten. *A Rosenberg by Any Other Name*. New York: NYU Press, 2018.

Jampel, Serena, and Yasmeen A. Khan. "'The White Man's College': How Antisemitism Shaped Harvard's Legacy Admissions." *The Harvard Crimson*. November 9, 2023.

Auletta, Ken. "Power, Greed and Glory on Wall Street: The Fall of the Lehman Brothers." *The New York Times*, February 17, 1985.

Shavit, Ari. *My Promised Land: The Triumph and Tragedy of Israel*. New York: Spiegel & Grau, 2013.

Foer, Franklin. "The Golden Age of American Jews Is Ending." *The Atlantic*, March 4, 2024.

Margalit, Yotam, and Neil Malhotra. "State of the Nation: Anti-Semitism and the Economic Crisis." *Boston Review*, May 1, 2009.

"Nearly Three-Quarters of Jewish Students Experienced or Witnessed Antisemitism on Campus, New Survey Finds." Anti-Defamation League, November 29, 2023.

"Audit of Antisemitic Incidents 2023 Highlights." Anti-Defamation League.

Chapter 5. Antisemitism, Technology, Social Change, and Social Media

"French Yellow Journalism." *The New York Times*, July 17, 1898.

Durkheim, Émilie. "Antisemitism and Social Crisis." 1899.

Somerville, Keith. *Radio Propaganda and the Broadcasting of Hatred: Historical Development and Definitions*. Palgrave Macmillan, 2012.

Streicher, Julius. "Speech on the referendum on November 12, 1933," in "Radio and the Rise of the Nazis in Prewar Germany," by Maja Adena, Ruben Enikolopov, Maria Petrova, Veronica Santarosa, and Ekaterina Zhuravskaya, 2013.

Goebbels, Joseph. "Speech in Frankfurt am Main during election campaign for the parliamentary elections on March 5, 1933," in "Radio and the Rise of the Nazis in Prewar Germany," by Maja Adena, Ruben Enikolopov, Maria Petrova, Veronica Santarosa, and Ekaterina Zhuravskaya, 2013.

"Reverend Charles E. Coughlin (1891-1979)." American Experience | America and the Holocaust. PBS.

"American Adults Express Increasing Anxiousness in Annual Poll." American Psychiatric Association, May 1, 2024.

U.S. Surgeon General. *Our Epidemic of Loneliness and Isolation*. 2023.

Haidt, Jonathan. *The Anxious Generation*. New York: Penguin Press, 2024.

Bonsaksen, Tore, Mary Ruffolo, Daicia Price, Janni Leung, Hilde Thygesen, Gary Lamph, Isaac Kabelenga, and Amy Østertun Geirdal. "Associations Between Social Media Use and Loneliness in a Cross-National Population: Do Motives for Social Media Use Matter?" *Health Psychology and Behavioral Medicine* 11, no. 1 (January 2023).

Interview of Arthur Miller, *The Observer*, November 26, 1961.

"News Platform Fact Sheet." Pew Research Center, September 17, 2024.

"Social Media Fact Sheet." Pew Research Center, September 17, 2024.

"The Dark Side of Social Media: How It Fuels Antisemitism." Brandeis University, May 13, 2022.

Dwoskin, Elizabeth, Joseph Menn, Naomi Nix, and Taylor Lorenz. "Antisemitism Was Rising Online. Then Elon Musk's X Supercharged It." *The Washington Post*, November 19, 2023.

"One in five young Americans thinks the Holocaust is a myth." *The Economist*, December 7, 2023.

Hübscher, Monika, and Sabine Von Mering, eds. *Antisemitism on Social Media*. Routledge, 2022.

Oremus, Will. "Bigots Use AI to Make Nazi Memes on 4chan. Verified Users Post Them on X." *The Washington Post*, December 14, 2023.

Simhony, Limor. *Regulating Online Harms: Tackling Anonymous Hate*. Anti-Semitism Policy Trust.

Oboler, Andre, Eliyahou Roth, Jasmine Beinart, and Jessen Beinart. *Online Antisemitism After 7 October 2023*. Caulfield South, Victoria: Online Hate Prevention Institute, 2024.

Chapter 6. Antisemitism on the Right

Thorne, Stephen J. "That Time They Held a Nazi Rally at Madison Square Garden." *Legion*, October 30, 2024.

Sander, Gordon F. "When Nazis Filled Madison Square Garden." POLITICO, August 23, 2017.

Kramer, Sarah Kate. "When Nazis Took Manhattan." *National Public Radio*, February 20, 2019.

Wodak, Ruth. "The Radical Right and Antisemitism." *Oxford Handbook of the Radical Right*, February 5, 2018.

Holland, Michael. "Eugenics and Immigration." University of Missouri Special Collections and Archives, 2011.

SOURCES

Ken Burns et al.. *The U.S. and the Holocaust*. PBS. 2022.

Black, Edwin. "Hitler's debt to America." *The Guardian*, February 5, 2004.

Allington, Daniel, David Hirsh, and Louise Katz. "Antisemitism Is Predicted by Anti-Hierarchical Aggression, Totalitarianism, and Belief in Malevolent Global Conspiracies." *Humanities and Social Sciences Communications* 10, no. 1 (April 10, 2023).

Lodge, Henry Cabot. "Speech before the Boston City Club," March 20, 1908.

Orth, Taylor. "Which Conspiracy Theories Do Americans Believe?" YouGov, December 8, 2023.

Lardner, George Jr. and Michael Dobbs. "New Tapes Reveal Depth of Nixon's Anti-Semitism." *The Washington Post*, October 6, 1999.

Murphy, Carlyle. "Jews Angry Over Remarks by Falwell." *The Washington Post*, January 22, 1999.

Foer, Franklin.

Brockell, Gillian. "'The father of 'great replacement': An ex-socialist French writer." *The Washington Post*, May 17, 2022.

Gabriel, Trip. "A Timeline of Steve King's Racist Remarks and Divisive Actions." *The New York Times*, January 15, 2019

Peoples, Steve. "Republican Senate candidates promote 'replacement' theory." *Associated Press*, May 17, 2022.

"Trump closing campaign ad revives remarks seen as striking anti-Semitic tones." *The Times of Israel*, November 6, 2016.

Green, Emma. "Why the Charlottesville Marchers Were Obsessed With Jews." *The Atlantic*, August 15, 2017.

"Full text: Trump's comments on white supremacists, 'alt-left' in Charlottesville." *POLITICO*, August 15, 2017.

Adkins, Laura E. and Emily Burack "Neo-Nazis, QAnon and Camp Auschwitz: A Guide to the Hate Symbols and Signs on Display at the Capitol Riots." *Jewish Telegraphic Agency*, January 7, 2021.

Schor, Elana. "Anti-Semitism seen in Capitol insurrection raises alarms." *Associated Press*, January 13, 2021.

Chapter 7. Antisemitism on the Left

Faber, Sarah W. and Vicki Xu. "Harvard's 'Marshmallow Revolution,' 50 Years Later." *The Harvard Crimson*, April 8, 2021.

Lambert, Craig. "Echoes of 1969." *Harvard Magazine*, March-April 2019.

SOURCES

Knieriem, Declan J. "'Haunted by the War': Remembering The University Hall Takeover of 1969." *The Harvard Crimson*, May 27, 2019.

"Confrontation in Harvard Yard." *LIFE Magazine*, April 25, 1969.

Hartocollis, Anemona, Jeremy W. Peters and Dana Goldstein. "Feeling Alone and Estranged, Many Jews at Harvard Wonder What's Next." *The New York Times*, December 16, 2023.

Smith, Tovia. "3 Columbia deans resign over texts that 'touched on ... antisemitic tropes.'" *National Public Radio*, August 8, 2024.

Marx, Karl. "On the Jewish Question." *Deutsch–Französische Jahrbücher*, 1844.

"Investigation into Antisemitism in the Labour Party." Equality and Human Rights Commission, 2020.

Fischbach, Michael R. "The New Left and the Arab-Israeli Conflict in the United States." *Journal of Palestine Studies* 49, no. 3 (May 1, 2020): 7–21.

"Financial Crisis Sparks Wave of Internet Anti-Semitism." Anti-Defamation League, October 24, 2008.

Hersh, Eitan and Dahlia Lyss. "A Year of Campus Conflict and Growth: An Over-Time Study of the Impact of the Israel-Hamas War on U.S. College Students." Jim Joseph Foundation, September 2024.

Alper, Becka A. and Alan Cooperman. "U.S. Jews' Connections With and Attitudes Toward Israel." Pew Research Center, May 11, 2021.

"Hamas in 2017: The Document in Full." *Middle East Eye*, May 2, 2017

"Hamas Covenant 1988." The Avalon Center at the Yale Law School Lillian Goldman Law Library.

Chapter 8. American Jews and Israel

Nortey, Justin. "U.S. Jews Have Widely Differing Views on Israel." Pew Research Center, May 21, 2021.

"Balfour Declaration 1917." The Avalon Center at the Yale Law School Lillian Goldman Law Library.

"United Nations Resolution 181." *Encyclopedia Britannica*.

Matthew, William. "U.S. Recognition of Israel, 14 May 1948. Part III: 'A Near-Run Thing.'" The Balfour Project, May 4, 2019.

"Jacobson, Edward Papers." Harry S. Truman Memorial Library and Museum.

Shavit, Ari.

SOURCES

Aronson, Geoffrey. "Soviet Jewish Emigration, the United States, and the Occupied Territories." *Journal of Palestine Studies* 19, no. 4 (July 1, 1990): 30–45.

Reeves, Phillip. "On Multiple Fronts, Russian Jews Reshape Israel." *National Public Radio*, January 2, 2013.

Keating, Joshua. "The Longshot Plan to End the War in Gaza and Bring Peace to the Middle East." *Vox*, May 3, 2024.

Alper, Becka. "How U.S. Jews are Experiencing the Israel-Hamas War." Pew Research Center, April 2, 2024.

Silberg, Mordechai. "History of the Jews of Czortkow."

Chapter 9. Antisemitism and Israel

Rosman, Katherine. "Columbia Bars Student Protester Who Said 'Zionists Don't Deserve to Live.'" *The New York Times*, April 26, 2024.

Soch, Jonathan. "Anti-Semitism on rise: Study finds 2014 was worst year for attacks since 2009." *The Washington Times*, April 15, 2015.

"Working Definition of Antisemitism." International Holocaust Remembrance Alliance.

Sachar, Howard M. *A History of the Jews in the Modern World. New York*: Vintage Books, 2006.

"High School Girls' Basketball Game Aborted in New York Amid Antisemitic Slurs." *The Times of Israel*, January 7, 2024.

Troy, Gil. *Moynihan's Moment: America's Fight Against Zionism as Racism.* Oxford: Oxford University Press, 2013.

"Definitions of Genocide and Related Crimes." United Nations Office on Genocide Prevention and the Responsibility to Protect.

Schama, Simon. "Antisemitism Then and Now." Aspen Ideas Festival, June 25, 2024.

Friedrichs, Jonathan. "Will the Exact Number of Jewish Victims Ever Be Known?" Vancouver Holocaust Education Centre.

Oxford English Dictionary, s.v. "genocide (v.), Etymology."

"Hybrid Threats: Hamas' Use of Human Shields in Gaza." NATO Strategic Communications Centre of Excellence, 2019.

Said, Summer and Rory Jones. "Gaza Chief's Brutal Calculation: Civilian Bloodshed Will Help Hamas." *Wall Street Journal*, June 10, 2024.

"Settler Colonialism." Legal Information Institute at Cornell Law School.

"1948 Arab-Israeli War." *Encyclopedia Britannica*.

SOURCES

Mifano, Andrea. "The Expulsion of Jews from Arab Countries and Iran – An Untold History." World Jewish Congress, February 2, 2021.

Broadcast, "New Rule: From the River to the Sea." *Real Time with Bill Maher,* December 15, 2023.

"The Oslo Accords and the Arab-Israeli Peace Process." U.S. State Department Office of the Historian.

Federman, Josef. "Abbas Admits He Rejected 2008 Peace Offer from Olmert." *The Times of Israel,* November 19, 2015.

Chapter 10. Conclusion

DellaPergola, Sergio. "World Jewish Population, 2021." *The American Jewish Year Book* 121 (2021): 313-412.

Joyce, James. *Ulysses.* New York: Vintage Books, 1990.

De Montaigne, Michel. "On Cruelty." *Essais,* 1580.

"Passover Haggadah." *The Venice Haggadah,* 1609.

Kerouac, Jack. *On the Road.* New York: The Viking Press, 1957.

Lichtenstein, Diane and Esther Schor. "Emma Lazarus." *The Shalvi/Hyman Encyclopedia of Jewish Women,* Jewish Women's Archive.

Chuck Schumer is the Senate Democratic Leader and highest-elected Jewish official in American history. He is the author of *Positively American: Winning Back the Middle-Class One Family at a Time.*

Josh Molofsky was Senator Schumer's chief speechwriter before writing for several high-profile figures, including the U.S. Ambassador to the United Kingdom. Raised in Connecticut, he is a graduate of Tufts University.